T0031951

When Bad Thinking
Happens to Good People

When Bad Thinking Happens to Good People

How Philosophy Can Save Us from Ourselves

Steven Nadler

Lawrence Shapiro

PRINCETON UNIVERSITY PRESS

PRINCETON & OXFORD

Published by Princeton University Press
41 William Street, Princeton, New Jersey 08540
6 Oxford Street, Woodstock, Oxfordshire OX20 1TR

press.princeton.edu

All Rights Reserved
ISBN 9780691212760
ISBN (e-book) 9780691220086

British Library Cataloging-in-Publication Data is available

Editorial: Rob Tempio and Matt Rohal
Production Editorial: Mark Bellis
Text Design: Karl Spurzem
Jacket Design: Amanda Weiss
Production: Erin Suydam
Publicity: Maria Whelan and Amy Stewart
Copy Editor: Beth Gianfagna

This book has been composed in Arno Pro and Neue Haas Unica

Printed on acid-free paper. ∞

Printed in the United States of America

10 9 8 7 6 5 4 3 2 1

Contents

Acknowledgments

We would like to express our gratitude to the wonderful editorial, production, and marketing teams at Princeton University Press, with special thanks to publisher Rob Tempio and associate editor Matt Rohal. We wanted to write a philosophical book that would be accessible to as broad an audience as possible, in the hope that it may do some good, and the encouragement, support, and expertise they offered us in our endeavor is greatly appreciated.

We are especially grateful to the many friends and colleagues—philosophical and otherwise, too many to name—who not only lent a patient ear as we developed our thoughts but also offered many useful questions, comments, and suggestions. Apparently, irrationality is an easy topic on which to engage people. Even the most casual conversations—many of which took place during long days in the saddle bicycling through the rolling hills of the Driftless Region of Wisconsin—were, in a time of medical, political, and environmental crisis, an invaluable opportunity to work through our ideas and gain new perspectives on reasonable and unreasonable thinking and behavior. Finally, special thanks to Elliott Sober, for his insightful reading of some of the chapters, and to our agent, Andrew Stuart, for helping us find the perfect home for the book.

When Bad Thinking
Happens to Good People

Introduction

Our Epistemological Crisis

Something is seriously wrong. An alarming number of citizens, in America and around the world, are embracing crazy, even dangerous ideas. They believe that vaccinations cause autism. They reject the scientific consensus on climate change as a "hoax." They think that hordes of criminals ("murderers and rapists," in the words of some politicians) are invading the United States through its southern borders. They blame the emerging 5G network for the spread of COVID-19. A growing movement of conspiracy theorists under the banner of "QAnon" espouses the idea that prominent politicians and movie stars are involved in a cannibalistic pedophile ring. Meanwhile, so-called Birthers continue to insist that the presidency of Barack Obama was illegitimate because he was not a "natural born citizen" of the United States. At the same time, a shockingly high percentage of American citizens continue to believe that Donald Trump really won the 2020 presidential election.

There is nothing to substantiate these beliefs, and easily available evidence shows that they are actually false. And yet, people—often educated, smart, and influential people—continue to believe them. The *New York Times* columnist and Nobel Prize–winning economist Paul Krugman has called them "zombie ideas": they continue to circulate despite being "dead," disproven, and refuted.[1] Even more troubling, the people who believe these things advocate for public policies that reflect their madness and vote for politicians who (whether they share those beliefs or not) promise to enact them. Especially remarkable is how these people come to hold beliefs and defend corresponding policies that, in fact, are contrary to their own best interests.

These are instances of "bad thinking." Examples can be multiplied and internationalized. Elections, referenda, policies, and movements, not to mention actions both innocent and criminal, in numerous countries around the world, testify to an epidemic of bad thinking. Our focus, however, will be on the country we know best and the citizens among whom we live and work.

In this book we explain why bad thinking happens to good people. We consider why so many people can go so wrong in their beliefs and, consequently, in their actions. The way they come to form and defend these opinions is wrong, and their failure to appreciate the moral consequences of acting on them is wrong. The philosophical subjects of *epistemology*, which addresses how beliefs become justified and how knowledge differs from mere belief, and *ethics*, the study of the moral principles that ought to govern our behavior, can help us understand the difficult and perilous situation in which we now find ourselves. We also suggest a way forward, away from all this madness, through the tools of philosophy—its questions, its methods, and even its millennia-old history of recommendations for how to lead a good, rational, and "examined" life.

A simple, if somewhat brutal, diagnosis of the current state of affairs in America is this: a significant proportion of the population are not thinking reasonably and responsibly.[2] The real problem is not that they lack knowledge, education, skill, or savvy. Acting on incomplete knowledge or without the requisite skills can doubtless lead to disagreeable consequences. However, a person who does so might be blameless—morally blameless, if she really could not have done otherwise, and even epistemically blameless, if she could not possibly have known better. We often have no choice but to act in ignorance of all the facts, the knowledge of which may be beyond our grasp, or when not adequately trained to meet a particular challenge. Similarly, we wish to distinguish what we are calling bad thinking from being unintelligent. Unintelligent people, who simply cannot figure out what to do or how to do it, no less than ignorant or unprepared people, might choose actions that end up doing more harm than good. But, like the ignorant or unprepared, unintelligent people might be blameless for their witless deeds. Few people, if any, are unintelligent by choice, and so blaming them for ill-conceived actions is often inappropriate.

On the other hand, bad thinking, as we understand it, *is* a character flaw deserving of blame. Unlike ignorance or lack of intelligence—and bear in mind that even very smart, capable, and highly educated people can think badly—it is generally avoidable. People who think badly do not *have to* think badly. They may be—or, at least, *should* be—perfectly aware that they are forming and holding beliefs irrationally and irresponsibly, and even doing so willfully. But they typically refuse to take the steps that would cure them of their condition. Some philosophers and psychologists have insisted that we really have very little control over what we believe, that the process of belief formation is not some voluntary process under the control of the will. Perhaps this is true for some of our beliefs, but it seems obviously *not* true for a good number of them, many of which are of great consequence for how we lead our lives and how we treat others. Bad thinking is a bad habit, and there is a remedy for it.

This book is directed at illuminating the various dimensions of bad thinking so that it might be more easily recognized and treated. As we show, the most potent antidote to bad thinking is the wisdom and insights, as well as the practical skills—yes, *practical* skills!—provided by philosophy and its history.

Bad Thinking as Stubbornness

Bad thinking is a kind of stubbornness, one that reveals itself in several ways. The first kind of stubbornness, exhibited by those who deny climate change, the theory of evolution, or the benefits of vaccination, is *epistemic*. You are epistemically stubborn when you fail to tailor your beliefs to evidence. Epistemic stubbornness is manifest anytime you refuse to change your belief even in the face of overwhelming evidence that it is false. The Americans whom surveys identify as holding untenable, even absurd, beliefs are engaged in this form of bad thinking. They obstinately retain beliefs that are not only unjustified by any reasonable standard, but that a fair inspection of available evidence reveals to be conspicuously wrong. With bad thinking, people believe what they want to believe no matter the rationality of the belief. There may indeed be reasons that explain why they hold onto to these false beliefs—perhaps the beliefs are comforting to them, or maybe the beliefs offer economic or personal benefits, or people they admire hold the beliefs in question—but these are not epistemic reasons that justify the belief, that count as evidence for the truth of the belief.

The other kind of stubbornness that is a part of bad thinking—and this brings us to the moral dimensions of the problem—shows itself in the exercise of poor judgment. Where the epistemically stubborn person holds on to a belief regardless of compelling reasons against it, the *normatively* stubborn person insists on following a rule no matter how obviously wrongheaded doing so is in present circumstances. Normatively stubborn people fail to recognize when an exception to the rule is not only perfectly harmless but even leads to some good or the prevention of something bad.

People who engage in bad thinking are stubborn. They are epistemically stubborn when they hold on to beliefs in the face of overwhelming evidence that the beliefs are false and when they refuse to endorse beliefs in the face of overwhelming evidence that they are true. They are ethically or normatively stubborn when they insist on following rules irrespective of the intent that motivated creation of the rule in the first place or the benign or beneficial consequences of allowing an exception. Moreover, insofar as stubbornness is willful—under your control—bad thinking is blameworthy in a way that being ignorant or unintelligent is often not. Bad thinking is always avoidable.

Treating Stubbornness

But how can an epistemically stubborn person come to see that his beliefs should be abandoned? How can the normatively stubborn rule-follower acquire powers of reasonable judgment? An important first step toward eliminating the stubbornness that marks bad thinking is an appreciation for the logical principles that guide philosophical and scientific thought and the norms that make for rational thinking. The cure for bad thinking is, naturally, learning how to think well. And thinking well involves knowing and following the canonical standards of rationality that lead to the responsible formation and defense of beliefs. In other words, it means both knowing how to know, as well as putting that knowledge about knowing into practice.

There is, in fact, an ancient name for this antidote to epistemic and normative stubbornness: wisdom. As Socrates, Sophocles, Plato, Aristotle, and a host of other thinkers and writers understood it, wisdom is a kind of self-knowledge. The wise person knows what she knows and, just as important, what she does not know. Moreover, the wise person takes care to ensure that her choices and actions are informed and guided by this self-knowledge. Fully aware of the extent and limitations of her knowledge, she thereby also knows what to do and what not to do. In short, the wise person is reasonable in thought and in action. As a result, the life she leads—what Socrates called an "examined life"—will be the best kind of life for a human being. It will consist in a kind of human flourishing. The ancient Greeks had a term for this as well: *eudaimonia*, inaccurately but not unreasonably often translated as "happiness."

Rational Enlightenment

In approaching the problem of epistemic stubbornness, it pays to remember that we are, for better and for worse, heir to the intellectual legacy of early modern Europe. What characterizes philosophy and science in this period and marks a break from earlier traditions is the concern to tailor theories to evidence rather than authority or tradition. Galileo Galilei, Francis Bacon, René Descartes, Baruch Spinoza, John Locke, Isaac Newton, and others formulated explanations of the heavens, of the natural world around them, and of human nature and society not by appealing to the proclamations of earlier thinkers (such as Plato and Aristotle). Nor were religious principles and ecclesiastic dogma their guiding lights. Rather, they took their lead from reason—what some thinkers called "the light of nature"—and experience. Whether they proceeded according to the logic of deduction or through the analysis of empirical data, the modern scientific method they developed consists in testing theories according to the strictures of reason and in light of the available evidence. A rational person seeks justification when evaluating the truth of his beliefs; he does not accept a belief as true merely on faith or because he really wants or needs the belief to be true; and when the evidence falsifies his beliefs, he abandons them. It is irrational—*just bad thinking*—to hold on to beliefs when they are plainly contradicted by the evidence or to reject beliefs when they are sufficiently justified.

These early modern thinkers were not irreligious men; many of them were deeply pious believers, devoted to the Catholic Church or one of the Protestant faiths. The alleged "war" in the early Enlightenment between science and religion is a myth. But for Descartes and his intellectual colleagues, philosophical, scientific, even moral and political truth and progress were a matter of rational and empirical inquiry, not fealty to authority, religious or otherwise.

People who reject climate change or who decline to vaccinate their children or who deny evolution by natural selection are not thinking well because in the face of relevant information they have refused to adjust or abandon their beliefs accordingly. Their commitments rest not on the "clear and distinct" evidence upon which Descartes and other early modern thinkers insisted but on prejudice, hearsay, and, of course, those unruly passions of hope and fear. Commenting on a recent trend, an article in the *New York Times* sounds the alarm against a federal administration that "has diminished the role of science in federal policymaking while halting or disrupting research projects nationwide, marking a transformation of the federal government whose effects, experts say, could reverberate for years. Political appointees have shut down government studies, reduced the influence of scientists over regulatory decisions and in some cases pressured researchers not to speak publicly."[3] The writers fail to note how much that aversion to scientific reasoning is deeply ingrained in American society generally and informs the decisions people make in their daily lives.

The philosophers of the early Enlightenment proposed, both in their codification of the scientific method and in their campaign against varieties of irrationality and groundless "enthusiasms," a systematic way of forming beliefs strictly on the basis of relevant evidence. Whether it is a matter of Bacon's inductive reasoning, Descartes's methods of "intuition" and "deduction," Newton's restraint in the face of speculative "metaphysical" hypotheses, or even David Hume's skepticism about our most ordinary but (it turns out) unjustifiable beliefs, all of these thinkers shared a commitment to a certain model of human rationality and epistemic responsibility.

This is not something that emerged all of a sudden in the seventeenth century. Plato was the first to investigate in a philosophically rigorous way the nature of "true knowledge" and the demands that we as responsible knowers are obliged to meet. And he was inspired to do so by his famous teacher. After all, it was Socrates who, with his well-known insistence that "the unexamined life is not worth living," urged upon us the obligation constantly to be asking ourselves not just why we act as we do, but why we believe what we believe. You think you know the meaning of justice? You have certain beliefs about the nature of right and wrong? The examined life demands not only that we reflect on our actions in light of our beliefs and values but that we put those beliefs and values themselves to the test.

Just as the insights of the Enlightenment trace back to a more ancient tradition, they also extend forward to contemporary work in philosophy. Philosophers who today investigate epistemology and science, no less than their early modern forebears, focus on questions concerning how evidence supports belief. They want to know how particular observations lend support to general claims about the world, and more generally how human knowledge works. In addition to the deductive and inductive tools first developed by earlier thinkers, contemporary philosophers incorporate as well the devices of probability theory. This provides them with new, more sophisticated means for understanding how well confirmed a belief may be, given some piece of evidence, and how, with additional evidence, the truth of a belief can become incrementally more probable. An understanding of these tools and methods can help even nonphilosophers spot spurious, invalid, or misleading arguments and unjustified conclusions, and can strengthen their thinking overall.

How to Think

What is the solution to our creeping epidemic of bad thinking? Arguably, the most promising response will involve a deeper engagement with philosophy: both its history and its methods. Take, for example, the field of epistemology. Learning how to gain more information from a broad variety of sources is an important first step. But we can all benefit even more from lessons in rationality. This means learning how to assess those sources of information—distinguishing between the real and the fake (that is, the *truly* fake)—and thereby acquiring the tools for determining which beliefs are likely true and which are likely false. We need, in fact, more lessons on what it means to be rational and how to be epistemically responsible citizens—citizens who care about truth, who can tell the difference between good and bad evidence, and who know an unjustified (and even unjustifiable) belief when they see one.

The basic rules of logic can go a long way in curing us of bad thinking. We can also look to more general rules that define rationality in order to understand errors that, once appreciated, can be easily avoided. Part of the therapy for bad thinking provided by philosophy is the practice in distinguishing good arguments from bad and in understanding how evidence supports or falsifies a principle or hypothesis. The goal is not to have anything but true beliefs—it is not about always being right. Being reasonable does not mean being infallible. Even the most epistemically responsible people will have false beliefs. But the reasonable person's belief, even if false, will be well-grounded. There will be good reasons why she has taken that belief to be true. And the reasonable person will, in the face of firm and incontrovertible evidence that contradicts his belief, abandon the belief rather than ignore or deny the evidence.

It is thus important to review the canons of rationality as these are expressed in the rules of logic and probability and, more generally, in the basic demands of responsible belief formation. This means understanding the difference between coming to believe something rationally versus coming to believe it as a matter of faith. Beliefs resting on faith need not be religiously momentous. Even the most mundane beliefs can be based on faith—for example, you can believe that a friend is good and trustworthy because all of her behavior justifies that belief, or you can believe that she is good and trustworthy even though you have no evidence whatsoever to support that belief, and maybe even evidence that she is evil and deceitful. If you believe that she is good without any evidence whatsoever, it is a matter of faith; if you believe that she is good despite the evidence to the contrary, then your faith is irrational.

There is too much irrationality in our country, and in the world.

Philosophy as a First Step

On May 6, 2020, the American Philosophical Society (APS) issued a rare public resolution in light of the COVID-19 pandemic. In its statement, the APS council expresses its concern that "rather than the deliberative, logical and analytical thinking that the country urgently needs, we find a disturbing skepticism toward evidence-based policy-making; a reluctance to accept and apply scientific knowledge; and a lack of familiarity with the relevant lessons of history, including long-past and more recent pandemics." The resolution, directed at the leaders of both houses of the United States Congress, concludes with the following recommendation:

> We therefore ask you to consider a bold initiative to re-energize education in this country as an essential part of the recovery from our current national emergency. This effort draws inspiration from the National Defense Education Act of 1958, a successful legislative initiative to support education in response to a clear international challenge.
>
> WHEREAS, Factual evidence and fact-based decisions are the foundation of the nation's strength and growth, and whereas, the promotion of education emphasizing the natural and social sciences, analytical thinking, and fact-based decision-making is essential for the nation's welfare, it is
>
> RESOLVED, That Congress enact a "National Defense Education Act for the 21st Century" to support at all levels the

education of American's youth in science, history, analytical thinking, and the primacy of facts as the foundation of the nation's future health, general well-being, and security.

Changing people's cognitive behavior will not be easy; it may even be a fool's errand. However, there is no reason to think that, just because old dogs have difficulty learning new tricks, people, too, once entrenched in bad ways of thinking, cannot come around to seeing the error in their ways. Perhaps it must fall to psychologists to investigate the best ways to incentivize good thinking among a population of bad thinkers. But it is the job of philosophers to identify which modes of thinking are good and why. This is why philosophy is fundamental to good thinking. If we are to cure America, and the world at-large, of the baseless and harmful ideas that have infected a frighteningly large portion of the population, it is to philosophy that we—as individuals and as a society—must first turn.

Chapter 1

Thinking, Bad and Good

In 2013, Fairleigh Dickinson University's PublicMind poll revealed that 25 percent of Americans believed that the Sandy Hook school shooting, which had occurred the year before, involved a cover-up of some sort. This skepticism—or, perhaps more accurately, cynicism—appears impervious to overwhelming evidence that, in fact, Adam Lanza murdered his mother before driving to Sandy Hook Elementary School, where he methodically killed six staff members and twenty children. The available evidence concerning Lanza's actions, including photographs of carnage, autopsy reports, witness testimonials, interviews with acquaintances of Lanza, disturbing material found on Lanza's computer documenting other mass shootings, and so on, should leave no doubt in a rationally functioning individual that the shooting did, without question, occur. Apparently, a large proportion of Americans are not functioning rationally.

Five years following the PublicMind poll, the online news source Patch published an article titled "How Dumb Is America: 10 Things People Actually Believe." Here are some of the actual beliefs that, according to Patch, suggest that America is, after all, pretty "dumb." Nearly one-third of Americans deny the historically established fact that approximately six million Jews were killed in the Holocaust, and instead insist on a far lower number. A still greater number of Americans do not even know that Auschwitz was a concentration camp. Seventy-four percent of Americans are unable to name all three branches of their own government, and an astounding one-third of Americans could not identify even a single branch of the government. A quarter of Americans believe that the sun orbits the earth. Over a third of Americans believe that human beings, rather than evolving through natural selection, were created by God in their present form, and not very long ago. While the number of Americans who accept the fact of climate change has been increasing, 20 percent of them still deny climate change, and an even larger percentage deny that human activity has anything to do with it. About a third of Americans continue to believe that President Obama was born in Kenya, and about a fifth are skeptical about the safety of vaccines, despite very large studies that show the incidence of afflictions like autism to be no higher in vaccinated populations than unvaccinated ones.

We prefer to resist the Patch article's description of Americans as "dumb." In our view, it is not the right word to describe America, or, more specifically, a discouragingly high proportion of Americans. Nor, to take a more global perspective, does it describe those around the world who similarly hold beliefs that fly in the face of overwhelming counter-evidence. However, we do agree with the general sentiment the article expresses. America's future—and the future of the world—is jeopardized by people who should know better. Not every false belief will have bad consequences—not much harm can come from believing that the earth is flat, unless, perhaps, you work for NASA—but many will. Climate change is real, and the longer people drag their feet responding to it, the more damage it will do. Similarly, the cost of avoiding vaccines is high. As the number of unvaccinated children grows, so too will the number of deaths that could have been prevented by a simple and easily procured inoculation. And those who deny horrific episodes like the Sandy Hook shooting should think hard about the parents of the slain children, whose misery they are cruelly compounding.

One reason why we do not like the word 'dumb' to describe the Americans that the Patch article singles out is simply that the word is insulting and thus unlikely to make its targets receptive to learning the skills that can help them understand why their beliefs are false or unjustified. But a more significant reason for avoiding the label is its inaccuracy. Many of the Americans who hold false beliefs are not in fact dumb. They did as well or better in school, or on standardized tests, as Americans who hold true beliefs. They may be able to defend their false beliefs with careful, articulate, and creative reasoning. There can be no doubt that proponents of the flat-earth hypothesis, for instance, have made a mistake in their reasoning somewhere, but a striking feature of this community is the cleverness of its misguided arguments.

Finally, in addition to being inaccurate, the adjective 'dumb' is unhelpfully imprecise. 'Being dumb' is simply too vague of a description to offer any insight into why Americans hold so many false beliefs or lack important true ones, thus making the path toward a remedy that much harder to follow. Looking more closely at some of the examples suggests at least two very different explanations for why Americans might insist on such blatant falsehoods or at least fail to recognize certain truths. Start with the observation that over a third of Americans do not know that Auschwitz was a concentration camp, and that about the same fraction cannot name a single branch of the US government. The explanation for ignorance like this is pretty straightforward. This group of Americans is poorly educated. They did not learn basic facts about the Holocaust or the organization of the government. Of course, the reasons why some Americans are poorly educated might themselves be quite complex, involving details about social and economic status, racism, geographical location, state budgets, tax rates, and so on. Nevertheless, whatever the reasons why some Americans are poorly educated, we can say that a failure to know that Auschwitz was a concentration camp, or that the US government is divided into three branches, is a product of poor education. The poorly educated simply do not know things that they should.

On the other hand, a person who denies that human beings have evolved by natural selection, or who refuses to admit that the earth is warming or that vaccinations are beneficial, or who sees a connection between the introduction of 5G networks and the spread of COVID-19 may not be poorly educated at all. Maybe this person attended very good schools and studied diligently. One prominent champion of the Sandy Hook cover-up story is an academic philosopher—a person who has spent his entire adult life associated with institutions of higher learning. Lack of education cannot be his excuse. What sort of deficiency leads these people to refuse to see the most rational conclusion to which clear and easily accessible evidence points? How should we characterize people who, while apparently normal and well educated in most contexts, display a bewildering irrationality when asked to think about global warming or vaccines or school shootings? These people could, and should, see their errors if only they were willing to properly weigh the evidence that tells against their false beliefs and in favor of the true beliefs. They are not dumb; rather, their bad thinking is an instance of *epistemic stubbornness*.

Stubbornness, Epistemically Speaking

Epistemology is the branch of philosophy that focuses on questions about justification and knowledge (*episteme* is the Greek word for "knowledge"). In characterizing someone as "epistemically stubborn," we are highlighting a particular sort of bad thinking. Stubbornness, we all know, involves a sort of resistance or defiance in the face of reason. The stubborn toddler refuses to give up her lollipop despite having dropped it on the beach. A person is epistemically stubborn when he refuses to give up his belief when readily available and easily acquired evidence—perhaps even right in front of his nose—reveals that belief to be false. Alternatively, he does accept the evidence but fails to draw from it the rational conclusion he should. Being epistemically stubborn is quite different from being poorly educated (and, for that matter, being dumb). A poorly educated or ignorant person may not know that Barack Obama is an American citizen just because she never saw any evidence one way or another about Obama's place of birth. An epistemically stubborn person, on the other hand, continues to deny that Obama is an American citizen despite seeing a copy of his birth certificate and hearing testimony that confirms his birth in Hawaii. Similarly, plain old ignorance might explain why someone has no understanding of evolutionary theory. But the creationist is typically deficient in another way. He is familiar with the evidence for evolution but either denies its relevance or refuses to accept what it entails. He is epistemically stubborn.

The instances of epistemic stubbornness that we have cited might seem correlated with particular segments of society—indeed, members of the Republican party are far more likely to be "birthers" than Democrats, and members of conservative religious groups are more likely to deny evolution than members of more progressive religious groups. However, epistemic stubbornness is not limited to populations who display profoundly partisan political views or sectarian religious convictions. Everyone is vulnerable to epistemic stubbornness at some time or another and with respect to at least some of their beliefs. Many sports fans continue to believe, well into a losing season, that their team can "go all the way." We have all met people whom we want to think have our best interests at heart despite a wealth of evidence to the contrary. Charlie Brown never lost hope that Lucy would keep the football in place for his kick. Epistemic stubbornness is without question pervasive. In some cases, as we will see, it might even be beneficial and desirable.

Yet, despite being common, and in many cases harmless, epistemic stubbornness can be dangerous, as is the case with climate change denial and vaccine skepticism. Other consequent evils of epistemic stubbornness might be less direct but just as insidious. Believing that a conspicuously flawed political candidate obviously unprepared and unfit for office can be an effective leader might lead a country down the wrong track or keep it from taking the right one. Buying into conspiracy theories involving the US government's involvement in the tragedy of 9/11 can hinder investigation into the real culprits and derail foreign policy that might prevent future terrorist attacks. When people give credence to the painful idea that prominent school shootings like Sandy Hook are fabrications—invented for the purpose of eroding gun-ownership rights—reasoned debate on important issues like gun control becomes ever more difficult.

The nineteenth-century mathematician and philosopher W. K. Clifford (1845–79) warned of an even more dire threat emerging from epistemic stubbornness. He worried that people who allow themselves to believe without sufficient justification are on a slippery slope. "Every time we let ourselves believe for unworthy reasons," he cautions, "we weaken our powers of self-control, of doubting, of judicially and fairly weighing evidence."[1] Epistemic stubbornness, the tendency to hold on to poorly justified beliefs, is, Clifford thinks, like a voracious contagion. It can take possession of a person, reducing her powers of discernment and making her "credulous"—in the sense that she will be prepared to believe almost anything, no matter how groundless. Her epistemic stubbornness can then spread to others, like a bad apple that spoils the barrel. "The danger to society," Clifford says, "is not merely that it should believe wrong things, though that is great enough; but that it should become credulous, and lose the habit of testing things and inquiring into them; for then it must sink back into savagery."[2] Perhaps the fear that an epistemically stubborn society will plummet into savagery is a bit over-the-top. But surely it is correct that a society that places no higher value on justified beliefs than it does on baseless ones is a dangerous place to live. We depend on society to protect us from enemies, to provide us with an education, to furnish us with adequate health care, to keep our environment clean, to ensure that the medicines we take and the food we eat and the houses and buildings in which we live and work are safe, and so much more. The last thing we want is for these essential operations to rest on unwarranted beliefs. And this is why understanding concepts like evidence, justification, and knowledge is important—it can help fight the spread of epistemic stubbornness.

Where Is the Evidence?

One very popular view in epistemology is called 'evidentialism,' and it tells us that people should believe something—that it will rain tomorrow, that the Pacific Ocean is larger than the Atlantic

Ocean, that Abraham Lincoln was president during the Civil War, that the atomic number of gold is seventy-nine—only when they have enough evidence to justify the belief. In other words, according to evidentialism, we ought *not* to believe something for which we lack sufficient evidence.

The historical roots of evidentialism can be traced back to the philosopher René Descartes (1596–1660). In his *Meditations on First Philosophy* (1641), Descartes set out to establish proper epistemological and metaphysical foundations for natural science. He was determined to discover a reliable method for arriving at absolutely certain truths about the cosmos. His first step toward this end was, ironically, an effort to doubt everything he believed. Yet skepticism—the view that knowledge is impossible—was not Descartes's goal. Rather, Descartes aimed to discover which of his beliefs could survive even the most powerful reasons to doubt. Among the reasons to doubt that Descartes considered was the possibility of an evil demon with God-like powers whose mission was to deceive him. Granting the existence of such a being, a forerunner to more contemporary skeptical scenarios such as the one appearing in *The Matrix* films, could Descartes trust any of his beliefs? Is the sun the center of the solar system? Is there even a sun? Does Descartes have a body, or is the demon making him believe that he does when in fact he does not? Does a square have four sides?

In imagining a reason to doubt everything, Descartes searches for and, he thinks, finds a reliable way to avoid false beliefs and enter the path to true knowledge. The key is to give "assent" only to what we "clearly and distinctly perceive to be true." That is, you ought not to believe something unless the evidence in favor of the belief is so overwhelming that it is practically impossible *not* to believe it. We should commit ourselves only to those things for which the evidence is so logically conclusive that we cannot resist believing them. At one point in the course of his epistemological progress, Descartes finds himself in the presence of certain ideas—he cites the thoughts "I am, I exist" and "God exists"—that were so compelling that "I could not but judge that something which I understood so clearly was true. This was not because I was compelled so to judge by any external force, but because a great light in the intellect was followed by a great inclination in the will, and thus the spontaneity and freedom of my belief was all the greater in proportion to my lack of indifference."[3] On the other hand, in the absence of such persuasive evidence—"in every case where the intellect does not have sufficiently clear knowledge"—we should withhold our assent. "If I simply refrain from making a judgment in cases where I do not perceive the truth with sufficient clarity and distinctness, then it is clear that I am behaving correctly and avoiding error."[4]

Clifford's version of evidentialism is equally strict. He sums up his position like this: "It is wrong always, everywhere, and for anyone, to believe anything upon insufficient evidence."[5]

Evidentialism, as we understand it, stands in direct opposition to the kind of bad thinking we are describing as epistemic stubbornness. The epistemically stubborn person essentially says, for example, "I will continue to believe that vaccinations are harmful despite the good evidence to the contrary," or "I still believe that the Sandy Hook school shooting was a hoax despite a mountain of evidence that the event actually occurred." An evidentialist views such an individual as violating a norm of some sort. Because the available evidence justifies the belief that vaccinations are not harmful, the antivaccination promoter has committed a kind of wrong. She has adopted a belief for which there is insufficient evidence; worse, she has adopted a belief for which there is compelling counter-evidence.

Likewise for the young-earth creationist, who insists that the earth is less than ten thousand years old. This person believes something on insufficient evidence, and even in the face of evidence to the contrary, and so, according to the evidentialist, has done wrong. The person who denies that children were killed at Sandy Hook is mistaken and ought to adopt different, better justified, beliefs about the events that occurred.

This brief discussion of evidentialism and its rejection of epistemic stubbornness raises many questions. The first set concerns the kind of wrong that epistemically stubborn people commit. When you believe something without having enough evidence to justify the belief, or refuse to abandon the belief in the face of overwhelming evidence that it is false, what have you done that is *wrong*? Of what offense, exactly, are you guilty? Can believing something without adequate justification ever be permissible?

A second set of questions concerns evidence: what is it and how much is enough to justify a belief? There are important distinctions between true beliefs, justified beliefs, and knowledge. It may come as a surprise that an epistemically stubborn person might be faulted for continuing to insist on a belief even when that belief is true. And a person who bases her belief on sufficient evidence might be praised for doing so even when that belief is false. The relationships between justification and true belief, and between true belief and knowledge, are not very obvious.

Two Kinds of Oughts

The dangers in allowing yourself to believe something without sufficient evidence or, worse, in the face of counter-evidence are easy to illustrate. Imagine a shipowner with nagging doubts about the seaworthiness of a ship he owns, which, with a full load of passengers, is soon to set sail. The ship is old, in need of frequent repairs, and not very well constructed in the first place. The evidence favors the belief that the ship is unsafe, and anyone not so invested in the ship as the owner would have seen this. And yet, through the sorts of mental contortions by which the epistemically stubborn refuse to see in which direction the evidence points, the shipowner convinces himself of the safety of the ship. As Clifford describes this example, the shipowner "said to himself that she had gone safely through so many voyages and weathered so many storms that it was idle to suppose she would not come safely home from this trip also."[6] But, of course, the belief into which the shipowner talks himself, that the ship could safely cross the sea, is false. "He got his insurance-money when she went down in mid-ocean and told no tales."[7]

Suppose that the ship had, despite its rotting wood and failing bilges, made it safely to its destination? Would we judge the shipowner any less harshly? He would no longer be guilty of manslaughter, as might be a reasonable charge when his neglect of the evidence was responsible for the death of the passengers. But, Clifford thinks, he is still guilty of something: "The question of right or wrong has to do with the origin of his belief, not the matter of it; not what it was, but how he got it; not whether it turned out to be true or false, but whether he had a right to believe on such evidence as was before him."[8] The shipowner's crime, in this view, is his readiness to believe something on insufficient evidence, with no real concern for whether the belief is true or results in bad consequences. And despite ample evidence to the contrary, he clings to his unjustified and self-serving beliefs. The wrongness attaches to the action of believing on the basis of insufficient evidence and in the face of counter-evidence, and the shipowner is no less guilty of this if his ship finds its way across the ocean without incident than if it ends up in at the bottom of the sea.

But there are different kinds of wrongs, and it would be good to know in what sense the shipowner is wrong when his belief rests on insufficient evidence. The most ordinary sort of wrong is associated with a *moral* infraction. If, instead of keeping your promise to pick up your friend at the airport, you instead sit at home watching reruns of your favorite sitcom, you have committed a moral wrong because you have broken a moral rule. Morality dictates that you keep your promises (unless, perhaps, some more important or urgent obligation presents itself). So, when you violate this moral rule, you behave immorally. You are, in short, morally wrong.

In contrast to a moral wrong, we can speak of an *epistemic* wrong. Suppose you believe that the zoo is open unless the workers are on strike, and you also believe that the workers are *not* on strike. If we then ask you whether you believe that the zoo is open, and you say "no" or "I don't know," you have committed an epistemic wrong. The first two beliefs justify the third. If you believe that the zoo is open unless the workers are on strike, *and* you believe that the workers are not on strike, then you ought to believe that the zoo is open. But this sense of 'ought' is not like the one that applies to the case of keeping your promise. When you ought to keep your promise and you do not, you have done something that, morally, you should not have done. When you ought to believe that the zoo is open but do not, you have failed to do something that, *epistemically*, you ought to have done. You have violated an epistemic norm, a norm of good reasoning.

Or, to consider another case, suppose your partner starts to receive text messages late at night and quickly hides the phone or leaves the bedroom when responding to them. He leaves the house often, saying that the dog needs a walk, despite the fact that the dog was sleeping soundly. Hidden beneath his side of the mattress, you find two tickets for a Caribbean cruise, the dates of which correspond to your annual work retreat. One of the tickets has been issued to your partner's business associate, with whom you have seen him flirting at various work functions. As the evidence of your partner's infidelity mounts, so does the justification for believing that he is cheating on you. Obviously, you do nothing *immoral* in refusing to believe the evidence, in sticking to the increasingly unlikely belief in your partner's innocence, but you do, as in the case above, break an epistemic norm. The evidence of your partner's infidelity is overwhelming. If you refuse to accept the belief that the evidence justifies, you are not believing what you ought, epistemically, to believe.

The two examples of epistemic wrongs we have just considered—not believing that the zoo is open and not believing that your partner has been unfaithful—differ in important ways. More specifically, the *manner* in which the reasoning in each case justifies a particular belief differs. We will see why in later chapters. For now, let us return to the discussion of the shipowner, because it suggests a connection between the two kinds of wrong that we just distinguished, that is, moral wrongs and epistemic wrongs.

Not every instance of epistemic stubbornness involves a moral transgression. You have done nothing immoral when you fail to see that the zoo is open. Nor, on the face of it, does your refusal to believe, despite all the evidence, that your partner is cheating on you make you a bad person. But the shipowner *is* a bad person. This is obvious in the first situation, when the shipowner willfully neglects the evidence that his ship is unsafe and sends its passengers to a watery grave. But matters are hardly less clear in the second situation, in which only luck spares the passengers from tragic misfortune. The ship is no safer in the second case, and the evidence for its decrepit condition just as compelling. The shipowner has acted immorally because he has put his passengers at grave risk when he should have known better.

In both cases—when the passengers drown, and when, by luck, they enjoy safe passage—the shipowner's morally wrong behavior is intertwined with his epistemically wrong behavior. His bad thinking prevents him from seeing the danger into which he is placing his passengers' lives. He convinces himself that the ship is seaworthy simply because his profits depend on doing so. Sometimes, as in this case, epistemic stubbornness acquires moral significance because failure to believe what you ought epistemically to believe results in actions that you ought morally to avoid.

To this point, we should add that although the shipowner has all the evidence in hand to justify the correct belief, that his ship is not seaworthy, he would be hardly less guilty if instead of having this evidence handed to him by shipwrights, he had to go to some effort to collect the facts. Given the serious stakes of an ocean voyage—the lives of many passengers—the shipowner has a moral duty to inform himself of the ship's true condition. Morally, the shipowner ought to do everything he can to assure himself that his belief in the ship's seaworthiness is justified. If he had done this, he would have realized that his belief was mistaken. Of course, he may well still have chosen to risk the lives of the passengers, but this would no longer be an instance of epistemic stubbornness. After all, he has now allowed the evidence to do its work—he allowed it to persuade him that his ship was unsafe. His crime, should he ignore the belief, would not be epistemic stubbornness but something more like negligence; he did know better, but acted with indifference to this knowledge.

The point of all of this is to make more explicit why the epistemic stubbornness that so many Americans display can also be morally wrong. Consider again two of our paradigm examples of this kind of wrongness: refusing to believe in global warming and refusing to believe that vaccines are safe. In each case, lives are at stake. Just as the shipowner should not ignore the evidence of his ship's dilapidation, and should, in fact, make every effort to seek evidence that justifies the correct belief about the ship's condition, so too should Americans work to educate themselves about climate change and vaccinations. The antivaccination campaigner, for instance, has a moral duty to acquire evidence for the correct belief about vaccines and to abandon the unjustified beliefs that lead to dangerous decisions. Children are dying because of the unjustified beliefs that are guiding the choices of those opposed to vaccination. Just as the shipowner's epistemic stubbornness leads to the immoral decision to send passengers on a perilous journey, so the epistemic stubbornness of the person opposed to vaccination leads to the immoral decision to needlessly risk the lives of children.

Of course, many participants in the antivaccination movement do believe that their decisions *are* justified, that they *are* evidence-based. You can imagine that the shipowner might also come to believe that his opinion of the ship's seaworthiness is justified. Perhaps he speaks to some passengers who had traveled safely on the ship years before and they assure him of its soundness. This reveals something important about the nature of evidence. As we will see, though, not all evidence is created equal. Or, put another way, some reasons to believe are not good reasons. Likewise, some evidence is persuasive only if other evidence is ignored.

We have already acknowledged that epistemically stubborn people are not always, in virtue of their epistemic stubbornness, immoral. The shipowner is immoral, as are those opposed to vaccinations and those who deny climate change. In each of these cases, a person refuses to accept the belief that the total evidence justifies, puts too much weight on poor evidence that confirms a contrary belief, and maintains a tight grip on that belief despite evidence that it is false, and all this bad thinking leads to decisions and actions that end up placing lives at risk. But refusing to believe that the zoo is open, or that your partner is cheating on you, leads to actions that do no harm to anyone (except, perhaps, to yourself in the case of the cheating partner). These examples of epistemic stubbornness seem to be morally neutral. They are like other cases in which a decision carries no moral significance: Should I walk to work or ride my bicycle? Should I eat an apple or an orange? Should I tie my left shoe or my right shoe first? Choices like these lack moral import because, roughly, they do not make contact with moral duties or obligations. No one is morally obliged to eat an orange, and so the choice to eat an apple instead is not a violation of a moral duty, as would be the case if you broke a promise or stole someone's wallet. Similarly, because epistemic stubbornness need not always have moral significance, Clifford's admonition that "it is wrong always, everywhere, and for anyone, to believe anything upon insufficient evidence"[9] cannot be correct if what is meant is that it is always morally wrong. As our examples illustrate, it is not always morally wrong to believe on insufficient evidence, even if it is always epistemically wrong to do so.

So far, in clarifying evidentialism—the view that you ought to believe something only when you have sufficient evidence—we have examined two ways to understand the meaning of 'ought.' The 'ought' might be epistemic, in which case evidentialism is the view that you have done something epistemically wrong when you believe something on insufficient evidence. You have committed an act of bad thinking. On the other hand, the 'ought' might be moral. From this perspective, epistemic stubbornness is immoral when it causes you to violate a moral duty or obligation of some sort, as does the shipowner and those who deny global warning or the benefits of vaccines. Our focus in this book is on evidentialism of this second sort. We deplore the kind of epistemic stubbornness that not only involves bad thinking but also leads to a moral failing. That is, we find fault with those who choose to believe on insufficient evidence when doing so leads to harm or increases the likelihood of harm. This makes especially valuable the lessons that we will be offering in subsequent chapters concerning how to think well. Taking them to heart can make you not only a better reasoner but a better person.

A Third Kind of Ought

Before turning to a discussion of what reasons are, and how reasons are related to concepts like justification, truth, and knowledge, we should think about an important objection to evidentialism. This will help clarify even further the more modest version of evidentialism that we defend. The objection to evidentialism we have in mind was most forcefully articulated by the philosopher and psychologist William James (1842–1910). One way to approach James's objection to extreme evidentialism is to think about whether, in addition to the epistemic and moral oughts that we have already discussed, there might be still another kind of ought that can be associated with beliefs. As we have seen, one reason that you ought not to believe on insufficient evidence is because canons of good reasoning proscribe against doing so. Another reason not to believe on insufficient evidence is because doing so might cause you to violate a moral duty. But to these epistemic and moral reasons to believe or not to believe something, there might be added another kind of reason that requires a third kind of 'ought.' We can call these reasons *prudential* reasons, and the kind of ought with which they are associated a *prudential* ought.

The idea behind the prudential ought is that sometimes it might be *prudent* to believe or not believe something, in the sense that believing (or not believing) either has some positive benefit for you or minimizes some harm to you. In such a case, we can say that you ought, prudentially, to believe (or not). The most famous example of the prudential ought comes from the philosopher and mathematician Blaise Pascal (1623–62). In his devout religious reflections, the *Pensées*, Pascal argues that even if the evidence for God's existence is not very strong, you should still believe in God.[10] Obviously, this is a conclusion that a strict evidentialist would strongly oppose. Why believe in God if such a belief lacks justification? How would such a belief differ from other unjustified beliefs, like those involving Santa Claus or the Abominable Snowman? Pascal reasoned that believing in God promises something like a very good return on a small investment. The cost of believing in God is not terribly great. And, if God exists and rewards those who believe in God with the eternal gift of heaven, then believing in God has a tremendous payoff. If, on the other hand, God does not exist, then, because the cost of believing in God is very small, you have not lost much. On the other hand, suppose you choose not to believe in God. If God does not exist, your decision not to believe in God might provide you with a very small benefit. Perhaps you can feel good about the time you did not waste in prayer or other forms of devotion. However, if you do not believe in God and God *does* exist, and if God punishes those who do not believe—as the Abrahamic religions typically claim—then your choice not to believe will have terrible consequences for you: you will be in very deep, eternal shit. The smart bet, or "wager" as Pascal's argument is now called, is to believe in God, because that is the belief that promises the greatest expected utility. So, you ought to believe in God: not because the belief in God is the one that the evidence most favors or that is most in line with what morality dictates, but because it is the belief that is most likely to maximize your well-being. It is the prudential thing to believe.

Naturally, Pascal's wager involves a singular sort of situation. Not every belief determines whether you spend eternity in heaven or hell. James, however, thinks that prudential considerations are enough to underwrite many other beliefs, that there are many beliefs that we ought, prudentially, to hold even when we lack justification for doing so.[11] James does not think that evidential considerations should never carry the day when deciding what to believe. But in certain narrowly defined circumstances—for instance, those in which we have no choice but to believe something and when a choice to believe might actually have an impact on whether the belief is true—we are warranted in believing on insufficient evidence. Examples of the sort James had in mind are easy to come by.

Suppose you are presently unemployed and, fortuitously, receive two job offers. You must decide which offer to accept. Remaining unemployed is not an option—you have bills to pay, mouths to feed, and so on. Thus, you are "forced" to choose between the two offers. Assuming that you will want to take the better offer, you must then try to justify the belief that Offer A is better for you, or that Offer B is. But it is quite possible that you simply do not have enough information on hand to justify the belief that Offer A is better than Offer B, or vice versa. Maybe each offer has various attractive features but also some undesirable aspects. Offer A will bring you to a city that you have always loved to visit, but the cost of living is quite high, and you have heard rumors of low morale among some of your potential colleagues. Offer B does not require you to relocate, and you are generally happy with where you live, but the prospects for advancement are not what they are with Offer A. Additionally, you have heard that the work environment associated with Offer B is a very congenial one and that the employees all express a great deal of contentment.

If you were to accept the demands of the strong brand of evidentialism, according to which you ought never to believe something on insufficient evidence, then you would end up refusing to believe that Offer A is better than Offer B or that Offer B is preferable to Offer A. The evidence in your possession simply does not justify either belief. In these circumstances, you may find yourself simply unable to choose either option, but choose you must. Moreover, rather than simply flipping a coin, you are better off, James thinks, committing to one belief or the other. You should "will" yourself to believe, for instance, that Offer A is superior. Doing so is likely to have a salubrious impact on your future. You now move to a new city to take up a new job feeling confident that Offer A was the better position. And in believing this, you may even *make* Offer A the better choice, because you can convince yourself that the features of the job that distinguish it from Offer B are more to your liking or more in keeping with your values. Despite not having justification for believing that Offer A is better than Offer B, you ought to do so anyway. It makes the decision easier and, perhaps, more likely correct. Adopting the belief can be justified on prudential grounds.

Once you see the basic structure of a case in which believing for prudential reasons seems appropriate—when a choice between two beliefs, neither of which rests on adequate justification, is forced upon you—other examples are not difficult to find. Suppose that your longtime partner finally pops the question. An answer is required of you. Keeping silent is not an option. But you may not be justified in believing either that you should or should not marry your partner. You say yes with no certainty that the marriage will not, like so many do, end in divorce. But, as with the competing job offers, you have to believe something. Moreover, believing that the marriage will succeed has an obvious prudential benefit. Entering a marriage with the conviction that it is the right choice will increase the likelihood that it *is* the right choice. Almost certainly, the marriage is more likely to last if you approach it with confidence rather than uncertainty.

Other examples illustrate even more clearly the prudential payoff that comes from willing yourself to believe something despite an absence of epistemic justification. Suppose that a person is diagnosed with terminal cancer. Her doctors patiently and compassionately explain to her the extent to which the cancer has metastasized, the diminishing effectiveness of the chemotherapy she has been receiving, the life expectancy that others in a similar stage of the disease experienced, and so on. The evidence justifies the belief that the cancer will kill her. If the patient were to ask the strict evidentialist what she "ought" to believe about her prognosis, the answer would be to go with the evidence. She ought to believe that she will soon be dead.

But from James's perspective, it still makes sense to ask whether such a belief is in fact the one that she ought to have. Of course, if "ought" were understood in its purely epistemic sense, then the evidentialist would be correct. The patient ought to believe that she is dying. Yet, if we recognize the possibility that prudential considerations might play a role in what we ought to believe, the idea that the patient ought to believe that she can beat the cancer seems quite plausible. Suppose that the positive attitude growing from such a belief increases the odds that the cancer will go into remission. If so, believing what the evidence tells against—that she will survive—makes her survival more likely.

This same pattern is present in other, less gloomy cases in which believing that you can succeed in some difficult task, a task with which you have a history of failure, makes your success more likely. The pole vaulter who has never cleared a certain height, and so is justified in believing that she cannot, will surely have a better chance of success if she believes that she *can* do it. A first-year culinary student may not believe that he will make it through the demanding curriculum, but believing that he can will surely improve his chances.

In all of these cases, even if the unjustified beliefs turn out to be false—the cancer patient does succumb, the pole vaulter always falls short, the culinary student drops out in the end— adopting them might still have had a positive impact. Perhaps the patient lived longer than she would have if she had simply acquiesced to the belief that the cancer would kill her. Or, perhaps her life ended just when the doctors predicted that it would, but her last months were happier because she refused to accept the belief that the evidence justified. Maybe the pole vaulter still managed a personal best, which would have been impossible if she had not believed she could jump even higher; and the culinary student's belief that he could make it through the program, though false, improved his sauces nevertheless.

In short, a strong version of evidentialism leaves no room for reasons to believe other than those dictated by epistemic considerations. You should never believe on insufficient evidence, even when you have no choice but to believe, as when considering job offers or marriage proposals, and even when believing can positively contribute to the truth of the belief or yield other benefits.

This is not the sort of evidentialism that we endorse. In some circumstances, you ought (prudentially) to believe on insufficient evidence; it is not essential that *every* belief must have sufficient justification. Likewise, believing on insufficient evidence is not always a moral failing. Rather, according to a proper and reasonable version of evidentialism, epistemic stubbornness—the refusal to allow epistemic reasons to shape your beliefs—is wrong when the beliefs it tolerates cause harm.

Belief, Justification, Truth

Any discussion of epistemic stubbornness and its opposite—evidentialism—requires an analysis of such important concepts as truth, knowledge, and, most important, justification. The evidentialist demands that you do not believe without adequate justification. But what exactly is justification? And how much is enough to justify a belief? When are you justified in believing something—for instance, that Abraham Lincoln was the sixteenth president of the United States? Do you also *know* that Lincoln was the sixteenth president? Can you be justified in believing that Lincoln was the seventeenth president although he was not? Can you *know* that he was the seventeenth president if he was not? And what supports our repeated claims that the beliefs of climate-change deniers and antivaccination proponents are unjustified? Does not the person who rejects vaccination have reasons for her false beliefs about the dangers of inoculation? If having reasons, whatever they may be, are sufficient to justify a belief, then her belief, though false, is not without justification after all. And if it is not without justification, then why say that it is not justified? In order to sort through these issues, we need to delve more deeply into what philosophers have to say about epistemology, the theory of knowledge.

Crucial to any discussion of justification is the idea that beliefs are the kinds of things that can enjoy some measure of support. We will use the terms 'evidence' and 'reasons' synonymously, as labels for the support that a belief might possess—with the caveat that the kind of reasons we have in mind are epistemic, rather than prudential, reasons. Prudential reasons, after all, do not speak directly to the truth of a belief but only to whether the belief is, in a sense, good for you. Epistemic reasons, on the other hand, *do* count directly toward, or support, the truth of a belief.

Beliefs are also the kinds of thing that can be true or false. Insofar as your goal is to have true beliefs (including the belief that some belief is false), and to avoid having false beliefs, you will want to find support for the truth of your beliefs. That is, you will want evidence or reasons for believing as you do.

Notice that in all of these respects beliefs differ from many other kinds of thoughts you might have. For example, in addition to beliefs, you also have desires. But desires do not behave as beliefs do. It makes sense to ask whether a given belief, like the belief that a pint of your favorite ice cream is in the freezer, is true. And when trying to determine whether this belief is true, you will consider the support there is for its being true. You will think about the evidence or reasons that speak in behalf of that belief. You remember purchasing the ice cream last night. Or your partner mentioned seeing ice cream in the freezer. Or you saw the ice cream earlier in the day when retrieving some leftovers from the freezer.

On the other hand, it makes no sense to wonder whether your desire for ice cream is true. We can wonder whether it is true that you *have* a desire for ice cream, but that is not the same thing as wondering whether the desire itself is true. This difference between beliefs and desires is based on the fact that beliefs are, in a sense, reports about how things are. They make claims—typically, claims about the world. The belief that a pint of ice cream is in the freezer is a report about the contents of the freezer. This report, like any other report about how things are, might be true or it might be false. Likewise, the belief that the earth is warming is a report about something happening to the earth. Sadly, it is a true report. Desires, on the other hand, do not report how things are but report how you want things to be. When you desire that there be ice cream in the freezer, you are not reporting that the freezer contains ice cream; rather, you are expressing a hope that there *is* ice cream in the freezer.

Because beliefs are reports about how things are, we can ask whether they are true or false. (Philosophers express this by saying that beliefs have a 'truth value.' Having a truth value does not mean that something is true but rather that it is either true or false.) This question about whether a particular belief is true returns us to the issue of justification. In seeking to determine whether a belief is true, you must acquire evidence or reasons that support the belief. This is what we mean by *justification*. Justification for a belief consists in evidence or reasons that support the belief—that increase the probability of the belief's truth. As you acquire more and more justification for the belief, you are in an ever-better position to say with confidence that the belief is true.

An illuminating contrast to justified beliefs are beliefs that you adopt on the basis of faith. The expression 'based on faith' is not really apt. It is a metaphor that tempts one to accept faith as a kind of *reason* that provides support for a belief: some people believe on the *basis* of evidence; others believe on the *basis* of faith. But a belief "based" on faith is not really based on anything. Faith is not justification for a belief, but an absence of justification. The person who is not convinced by any of the arguments for God's existence but chooses to believe in God on the basis of faith is, in essence, saying "there is no (epistemic) reason to believe in God, but I believe anyway." When you believe something "on the basis" of faith, you are engaged in a kind of wishful thinking. Believing something on the basis of faith is no different from believing something purely because you very much want it to be true.

Evidence, or epistemic reasons, on the other hand, *do* provide a basis for belief. A belief that rests on evidence *is* supported, in the sense that the evidence is relevant to its truth. As you add or subtract reasons to believe, the probability of the belief's truth varies accordingly. This is not the case with faith. A belief about which you have all the faith in the world, but *only* faith, is, for all you know, no more likely to be true than one in which you have little faith, or even no faith whatsoever. Faith—often a desperate desire that a belief be true—simply makes no difference to the probability that the belief *is* true. You can have great faith that your freezer will contain ice cream. But that makes no difference to whether, when you open the freezer door, you are likely to find any. If, on the other hand, you have good evidence for your belief that a pint of your favorite ice cream sits on a shelf in your freezer, your belief is justified. Your longing might soon be satisfied.

"So, Why Do You Believe *That*?"

Before going further, we should think about a crucial distinction involving justification. The distinction is between there *being* justification for a belief and someone's *having* justification for a belief. Behind this distinction is the idea that evidence for the truth of a certain proposition—that there is ice cream in the freezer, or that vaccinations are safe—might exist even if you are unaware of it. If your roommate has seen ice cream in the freezer, then there is evidence for believing that there is ice cream in the freezer. Of course, until you have spoken to your roommate, you may not be aware that she has seen the ice cream. The evidence is there, even if unknown to you. Then, once your roommate makes the happy announcement that she has seen the ice cream, you have justification for believing that it is in the freezer.

Likewise, for tens of millions of years there has been evidence for why the dinosaurs went extinct. This evidence was, as it were, biding its time until someone, Luis Alvarez, used it to justify his belief that an asteroid strike caused the extinction. The evidence was there, waiting to be discovered. The proposition that an asteroid killed the dinosaurs was justified even before Alvarez believed it, because even before he believed it, there was, for instance, a layer of iridium—asteroid dust—in the soil from about the time the dinosaurs went extinct. Then, once Alvarez made this discovery, the justification that was, literally, under foot, came into Alvarez's possession. For millions of years there was evidence for what Alvarez believed—that an asteroid impact killed off the dinosaurs—and then once Alvarez discovered this evidence, he had justification for his belief.

This notion of having evidence or justification for a belief involves a claim about a person. You *have* justification for believing something. There is evidence in *your* possession. On the other hand, the claim that a belief is justified is about a proposition: it is the claim that evidence exists in support of its truth. Putting these ideas together yields a simple observation: there might *be* justification for believing something even if you do not presently (or ever) *have* justification for believing that thing.

There might be evidence of ice cream in the freezer even if you are unaware of it. For about sixty-six million years there has been evidence that an asteroid destroyed the dinosaurs, but people had been unaware of it until about 1980. Of course, these two ways of talking about justification are related. If you *have* justification for believing that there is ice cream in the freezer or that an asteroid killed the dinosaurs, then there *must be* justification for believing that there is ice cream in the freezer or that an asteroid wiped out the dinosaurs. However, as we have just seen, the reverse is not true. There may *be* justification for believing that there is ice cream in the freezer—the ice cream is there to be seen, and your roommate has seen it—even if you do not *have* justification for believing that there is (you have neither opened the freezer nor had a chance to speak to your roommate). Had it not been for Alvarez's discovery, perhaps we would never have justification for believing that an asteroid doomed the dinosaurs even though the justification exists.

This distinction sheds additional light on the sort of epistemic stubbornness to which we are objecting. Epistemically stubborn people, as we are conceiving them, *have* justification for the correct beliefs—that vaccines are safe, that President Obama is a US citizen, that the climate is changing as a result of human activity—but refuse to acknowledge it or take it into account. Unlike the case where there is justification for believing that there is ice cream in the freezer but you are unaware of it, and so you do not have justification for believing it, epistemically stubborn individuals do have the evidence they need to justify the correct beliefs, but they ignore it or deny it. They continue to doubt that there is ice cream in the freezer even after the roommate insists that the ice cream is there and even reveals a sales receipt for the purchase of the ice cream and photographs of it sitting in the freezer. They have seen the iridium in the soil and the crater off the coast of the Yucatán Peninsula but still deny that an asteroid wiped out the dinosaurs. In these cases, there *is* justification for the belief and the person *has* justification for the belief, but the person nevertheless stubbornly persists in rejecting the reasonable conclusion.

Because our concern is with combatting epistemic stubbornness, we will focus on issues concerned with *having* justification for believing. We are much more interested in what people ought to believe given that they have justification for a belief than we are with whether justification for a belief exists in the first place. We can adopt this attitude because the sorts of beliefs with which we are concerned—that vaccines are safe, that the earth is warming, that the Sandy Hook shooting occurred, that the spread of COVID-19 is unrelated to 5G technology—*are* justified. There is probably more justification for these beliefs than there is for the belief about the ice cream in the freezer, even given the eyewitness testimony, the sales receipt, and the photograph of the ice cream on the freezer shelf. The issue, then, is what to say to people who have justification for these beliefs but deny them nevertheless.

Are You Justified?

Once we concentrate on the idea of having justification for believing something, the next issue concerns a distinction that is often expressed colloquially between *having* justification (or reasons, or evidence) for believing something and *being* justified in believing something. Imagine, for instance, that you are a detective in search of a murderer. Your investigation has led you to a prime suspect. In developing a case against him, you must look for evidence that he is indeed the murderer. You seek to justify your belief that he murdered the victim. You find this suspect's fingerprint on a coffee table at the scene of the crime. This evidence, all on its own, is not enough to convince you that he is the murderer, but it adds support to your belief that he is. We can say that the evidence provides some justification for the belief, even while it does not make you justified in believing that he is the killer. You *have* justification for believing that the suspect is the murderer, but you are not yet *justified* in believing that he is the murderer.

In speaking this way, we are drawing attention to the idea that evidence can add or contribute to the justification of a belief while still not making the belief justified. However, the difference between having justification and being justified is merely one of degree. In the former case, we might speak of being *partially* justified in believing something, for instance, that the suspect is the murderer. Then, as you build the case against your suspect, perhaps you find additional pieces of evidence, additional justification, for believing that he is the murderer. The ballistics report shows that the bullet in the victim's heart came from the suspect's gun; witnesses saw the suspect leaving the victim's apartment shortly after hearing gunshots; friends of the victim say that she and the suspect had recently (and unamicably) ended a relationship. Each piece of evidence adds to the justification of your belief that your suspect is indeed the murderer. But it is not until you have accumulated enough evidence, enough justification, for your belief can we say that you are justified in believing it. Only then has the partial justification you originally had for believing in the suspect's guilt increased to the point where your belief is *sufficiently* justified. The difference between having justification for believing something and being justified in believing something is thus just one of degree. When you are justified in believing something, the amount of justification you have for your belief has crossed a threshold. It now suffices to warrant the claim that your belief is justified.

With the distinction between partial and sufficient justification for believing, we can now make sense of an earlier claim. We conceded that some epistemically stubborn people may well have justification for their beliefs. An antivaccination activist, perhaps, might support her position by pointing to an instance in which a vaccinated child is subsequently diagnosed with autism. All by itself, this fact hardly makes the belief that vaccinations are harmful justified, but it does partially justify, in the sense of providing some evidence for, the belief that they are harmful. If you have doubts about this, consider the difference between two responses that the antivaccination activist might make when you ask her why she believes that vaccines cause autism. One response is this: she says that the child was diagnosed with autism after being vaccinated. Alternatively, suppose she says that the child yawned after being vaccinated. The second response will probably leave you scratching your head. How does the fact that the child yawned support the belief that vaccines are harmful? Whether a child yawns after being vaccinated seems completely irrelevant to whether vaccines are harmful. But this just reveals why the antivaccination activist's first response—that the child developed autism after being vaccinated—is one that provides some justification for believing that vaccinations are harmful. It is relevant to an evaluation of the belief. If you doubt the connection between vaccinations and autism, you would feel compelled to explain why her evidence of a connection is not sufficient to justify her belief that the connection is real. On the other hand, you would not bother to take these steps had she made the remark about the child yawning after the vaccination, because no one in his or her right mind could think that a yawn is evidence that vaccinations are harmful.

Given that many of the beliefs to which epistemically stubborn people cling are not without some amount of justification, does this mean that they are not epistemically stubborn after all? Is the shipowner not epistemically stubborn if he possesses some reasons for believing that his ship is safe—it has made the passage successfully before, the ship looks okay, a fortune-teller has promised him that the ship is seaworthy? And yet, merely having reasons—even reasons that partially justify a belief—is not enough to prevent one from being epistemically stubborn. There are reasons, and then there are reasons. The epistemically stubborn person refuses to consider the right kinds of evidence, preferring those reasons, however inadequate, that support his favored belief. He holds tightly to his beliefs despite the presence of better reasons to give them up. But what are the right kinds of reasons? What are the reasons that make a belief justified rather than simply justify a belief?

The Right to Believe

Reasons, or evidence, offer support for a belief only if, most fundamentally, they are relevant to whether the belief is true. We saw this in the example of the antivaccination proponent who mentions a child who is diagnosed with autism after receiving a vaccination. The autism diagnosis is relevant to the truth of the belief that vaccinations are harmful because, given this diagnosis, we have more reason than before to suspect that vaccinations are harmful. Another way to make this point is to imagine that we have no preconceived ideas about whether vaccinations are harmful. When, however, we are told that a child was diagnosed with autism after being vaccinated, we now have some grounds for thinking that vaccinations are harmful. On the other hand, the fact that a child yawns after being vaccinated is irrelevant to the antivaccination belief. Yawning is not, in any sense, a harm; and so the child's yawning after receiving a vaccination gives us no reason to believe that vaccinations are harmful. If we start with a neutral attitude about the harmfulness of vaccines, being told that a child yawned after being vaccinated does nothing to shift us from this attitude.

Evidence in favor of a belief must be relevant to the belief's truth, but evidence *against* a belief must also be relevant to its truth. This idea is not so strange as it might initially sound. Suppose that an extensive study of vaccinated children shows that they are no more at risk for autism than unvaccinated children (and this is precisely what studies do show).[12] This is not evidence *for* the antivaccination belief, but it is relevant to the belief's truth. We can say that it is evidence that bears on the belief, and it does so by making the belief less plausible. Clearly, we should want to know facts such as those about the long-term effects of vaccines when deciding whether to believe that vaccines are harmful, and this is why such facts count as evidence, regardless of whether they confirm or disconfirm the antivaccination belief.

Matters become more complicated when we consider the various factors that go into judgments of relevance. Among these factors are other beliefs or background knowledge that are present or available to an individual. Philosophers often insist that, when seeking to justify a belief, you consider your *total* evidence for the truth of the belief. To see why, imagine again that you are a detective searching for a murderer. You have found the suspect's fingerprints on the coffee table, the ballistics lab has confirmed that the bullet in the victim's heart was fired by the suspect's gun, and you have interviewed witnesses who tell you that they saw the suspect leaving the victim's apartment after hearing gunshots. All of this evidence supports your belief that the suspect is the murderer. If you considered only this evidence, you might decide that the time has come to charge the suspect with the crime. But suppose you believe other things that, when taken under consideration, *defeat* the power of the above evidence to implicate the suspect—for example, the suspect has a credible alibi indicating that he was nowhere near the victim when the crime occurred. Your belief that he is the murderer may be justified if you ignored these "defeaters," but once you take into account your total evidence—everything you believe that is relevant to whether he murdered the victim—you may need to think about other suspects.

When epistemologists talk about "defeaters," they typically distinguish between those that *undercut* a reason to believe something and those that *rebut* a reason to believe something.[13] An undercutting defeater acts to undermine the relevance of a piece of evidence to a given belief. You have the suspect's fingerprint on the coffee table, the results of the ballistics investigation, and the damning testimony of the witnesses. But suppose you also happen to know that the suspect was a frequent guest of the victim's, and so finding his fingerprint on her coffee table is not unexpected. This fact undercuts the relevance of the fingerprint: the print loses its relevance because we are no longer surprised to find it on the victim's coffee table. Similarly, if you happen to know that the suspect recently lost his gun, or loaned it to a friend, then this knowledge undercuts the relevance of the ballistics report to your belief that he murdered the victim. What once had seemed like compelling evidence in favor of the belief that the suspect is the murderer now seems less so. Furthermore, if you have reason to believe that the witnesses were angry with the suspect about a debt he had failed to repay them, this too undercuts the power of their testimony to implicate him. In each case, an undercutting reason should weaken your commitment to a belief in which you might once have had great confidence.

Undercutting defeaters, in short, are facts that weaken the power of evidence to confirm a belief. Notice, though, that the undercutting defeaters that we just considered do not make it impossible for the suspect to be the murderer. Despite evidence that he lost his gun or gave it to a friend, he may, prior to the murder, have located or retrieved it. Similarly, although the witnesses may have been lying about hearing gunshots and seeing the suspect run from the apartment, they may also have been telling the truth. Rebutting defeaters, on the other hand, are facts that speak directly against a belief and in favor of a contrary belief. If you come to learn that the suspect was indeed two thousand miles from the scene of the crime, then he cannot possibly have murdered the victim. Similarly, if the suspect had been in a car accident a few hours before the crime was committed and was in a medically induced coma, then, again, he cannot have been the culprit. In both cases, we have evidence that rebuts the belief that this suspect is the murderer. He cannot have done so if he was nowhere near the scene or in a coma.

The demand that you consider your total evidence when seeking to justify a belief should now make more sense. When you are looking for evidence against the suspected murderer, it will not do to consider only the evidence that favors the belief that he committed the crime. If you are aware of circumstances that defeat the positive evidence, either by undercutting or rebutting it, then this information too must be brought into the calculation. It would be bad thinking to remain committed to a belief that has been undercut or rebutted. Likewise, the shipowner might very well have been justified (to some extent) in his belief that his ship was seaworthy if he had considered only some of the facts that were relevant to the safety of the ship. But had he considered his total evidence, he would have seen a number of defeaters that undermined or rebutted his belief. True, the ship had made the voyage successfully in the past, and this is evidence that it will do so again. But undercutting this positive evidence are reports from the shipwrights, who have spotted areas of rot in the ship's hull. Or perhaps the shipwrights have offered a rosy assessment of the ship's condition. However, this evidence in favor of the ship's seaworthiness is undercut by the knowledge that the same shipwrights were often negligent and had recently offered a similar report on a ship that subsequently sank.

When global warming skeptics and antivaccination proponents refuse to consider their total evidence and focus only on those facts that confirm their favored beliefs, they are exhibiting epistemic stubbornness. They are so committed to their own position, so stubborn in thinking that they must be correct, that they consider only the evidence that supports their view and not the evidence that defeats it. We will see that there is a name for the kind of mistake that occurs when you disregard your total evidence and attend only to those pieces of evidence that justify a particular belief. The mistake is described as a 'confirmation bias,' because it involves a bias *in favor* of some evidence—that which confirms your belief—and *against* other evidence that might undercut or rebut your belief. In order to avoid the confirmation bias, you must consider all of your evidence, whether it supports your view or not.

An interesting corollary to the idea that you must examine your total evidence when seeking justification for a belief is this: what counts as evidence for a belief may vary from person to person. This is true because your total evidence is relative to your background knowledge. If you know things that someone else does not, then something that is evidence for you may not be evidence for someone else; or something that is not, or is no longer, evidence for you may continue to be evidence for someone else. If you know that the suspect had loaned his gun to a friend, then the ballistics report no longer offers as much justification for your belief that he is the murderer. However, if the other detective on the case does not know about the friend, then she is likely to think that the report provides very strong evidence for the suspect's guilt. If she comes to learn, as you have, that the suspect had loaned his gun to someone, she now grants the ballistics report the same low evidential status that you do. Later, she learns something you do not know: the gun was returned to the suspect. The ballistics report once again justifies her belief that the suspect is the killer, while you continue to dismiss its evidential significance. Likewise, a shipwright's glowing report may justify one shipowner's belief in the safety of his vessel, but a similarly positive report may fail to justify the same belief for a shipowner who is aware of the shipwright's reputation for incompetence or deception.

The point that justification is relative to background knowledge connects with our moderate variety of evidentialism. If, according to moderate evidentialism, it is wrong to believe on insufficient evidence when the resulting beliefs produce harm, then you have a duty to acquire as much evidence as you can about topics like global warming and vaccinations when forming your beliefs about these issues. When disease spreads through a community of children, the antivaccination proponent cannot absolve herself of responsibility by claiming that her lack of background knowledge prevented her from appreciating the evidence against her belief in the harmfulness of vaccinations. Information supporting the positive value of vaccinations is readily available and has been for decades. In a few seconds one can find on the Internet descriptions of large-scale studies that show the incidence of autism to be the same in populations of vaccinated and unvaccinated children, and this result should put to rest suspicions about a causal link between vaccines and autism. The bad thinking that prevents people from accepting evidence like this is unpardonable. Similarly, the climate-change denier who continues to focus only on a small portion of his total evidence while the earth heats up around him is epistemically and morally reckless. Evidence that supports belief in climate change is easy to come by. You do not need any specialized education or advanced intelligence to understand it. Only bad thinking prevents climate-change deniers from seeing how the total evidence available to them undercuts or rebuts the justification they offer for their beliefs, thereby posing a dire threat to future generations.

We can summarize these points in the following way: in justifying a belief, you must cite evidence or reasons that support the belief. Something counts as evidence or reason for a belief only if it is relevant to the belief's truth. But in deciding whether and to what extent some information is relevant, you must place it in the context of other things you know or believe. Sometimes your background knowledge will add to the strength of a piece of evidence; other times it might undercut or rebut a piece of evidence. People might disagree about the amount of support a piece of evidence provides for a belief because they differ in their background knowledge.

Believing versus Knowing

Providing justification for a belief is, in fact, quite easy. Only the slightest bit of imagination is needed to say something relevant to whether a belief is true. We can, for instance, provide some justification for the belief that the earth is flat simply by pointing out that, when looking at the horizon from where you stand on the seashore, it *looks* flat. The appearance of the earth's flatness is partial justification for believing that it is flat, because whether it appears flat is relevant to whether it is flat. After all, you would expect the earth to look flat if it were flat, and to look some other way if it were not (although, of course, if you are standing on a very large sphere it will look flat!). Nevertheless, it remains true—and should be obvious—that this partial justification for the belief falls well short of providing sufficient justification for the belief.

Even granting this, however, you may still wonder when it is legitimate to go from saying that there is some justification for a belief to saying that there is sufficient justification for a belief. At what point do you move from having justification for believing something to being justified in believing it? In your investigation of the murder, you collect more and more evidence justifying your belief that the suspect is the killer. Eventually you decide you have amassed enough evidence to make your belief in his guilt justified. But how much evidence is enough? If you were the prosecuting attorney assigned to the case, what would you say to convince a jury that not only is there some justification for believing that the suspect is guilty, but that there is sufficient justification? And could you ever acquire enough evidence to say not only that you are justified in believing that he is the murderer, but that you in fact *know* that he is the murderer? Similarly, how might you respond to the shipowner if, in defending himself, he insists that while there may have been some justification for believing that his ship was unsafe, there was not enough to justify the belief that it actually was? How much is enough evidence to justify the belief that the ship is unsafe? When, if ever, is there enough to *know* that the ship is unsafe?

Answers to such questions are, unfortunately, not exact. Philosophers, no less than ordinary folk, disagree about how much justification is required to make any particular belief justified and how much justification is required to be able to say that you *know* something. But even granting differences of opinion over these issues, it is useful to review some basic relationships between justification, truth, and knowledge.

We can begin with a point we have already noted. Justification is something that is supposed to increase the probability that a belief is true. A belief with justification is more likely to be true than a belief without justification. If you have evidence or reasons for believing that it will snow tomorrow, or that the battery is nearly dead, or that iron is magnetic, then each of these beliefs is more likely to be true than if you had no evidence or reasons for believing them. You can think of justification as something like a quantity that can come in degrees: the more of it that a belief possesses, the more probable it is that the belief is true. This is one difference, as we have seen, between believing on the basis of evidence and believing on the basis of faith. Have as much or as little faith in a belief as you wish; that makes no difference to how likely it is that the belief is true.

But although justification increases the probability of a belief's truth, it does not *guarantee* its truth (except, as we will see, when the justification involves a certain kind of logical argument). That is, we can speak coherently of very well justified but nevertheless false beliefs. Similarly, it is perfectly sensible to speak of very poorly justified but nevertheless true beliefs. Justification does not, after all, make a belief true. A belief is true not *because* it is justified but because it happens to make an accurate report about the way things are. The belief that the car battery is nearly dead will be true only in the case that, as a matter of fact, the battery *is* nearly dead. The idea of justification concerns whether you *ought* to believe that the battery is nearly dead. If it is true that the battery is nearly dead, and if you have a lot of evidence for believing that it is nearly dead—the engine has trouble turning over, or the gauge reads close to zero—then it turns out, in this case, that the justification has not misled you. Epistemically, you are believing what you ought to believe, and what you ought to believe is true.

Sometimes, however, justification can deceive. The fingerprint on the coffee table, the ballistics report, the testimony from witnesses—all of this justifies your belief that the suspect murdered the victim. But because justification does not make a belief true, we can still ask whether it is true that he is the murderer. The belief that he is the murderer is more likely to be true given that it is justified than if there were no justification for it at all. But even when enjoying a huge amount of justification, a belief may still be false. Perhaps the suspect's nemesis has framed him. He has invited the suspect to the victim's apartment so that his fingerprints would be on the furniture; he has stolen the suspect's gun so that the ballistics report would identify him as the owner of the murder weapon; and he has paid people to lie about seeing him run from the victim's apartment. Because you are unaware of this nemesis's efforts to implicate the suspect, your total evidence does not include any of these facts. Given what you know, you believe that the suspect is the murderer. Your belief is justified but false.

The victim's sister, however, is convinced that it is in fact this scheming nemesis who has murdered the victim. She puts no stock in the idea that the original suspect is the murderer. She is aware of the evidence that justifies your belief in the suspect's guilt but dismisses it. Instead, she has hired a clairvoyant who assures her that the suspect's enemy in fact is the killer. The sister's only reason for believing that the nemesis murdered the victim is her clairvoyant's say so. Of course, the soothsaying of a clairvoyant is not to be trusted. It offers terrible justification for believing anything. Consequently, the sister's belief that the suspect's nemesis murdered the victim, even if true, is unjustified (or, at any rate, very poorly justified). The victim's sister, in this case, has an unjustified but *true* belief (in contrast to your justified but *false* belief).

That justified beliefs may be false, and unjustified ones true, suggests a way to distinguish justified belief from *knowledge*. Intuitively, when you claim to *know* something, you are saying something stronger than when you claim to be justified in believing something—just as when you claim to be justified in believing something you are saying something stronger than when you claim simply to believe something. You can believe that your suspect is the murderer without being justified in the belief; and you can be justified in believing that he is the murderer without *knowing* that he is. The difference between merely believing something and being justified in believing something should now be familiar. Your belief is justified only when you have evidence or reasons that are relevant to whether the belief is true. But what is the difference between being justified in believing something and knowing it?

To address this question, we need to return to an earlier question concerning the difference between having some justification for a belief and having sufficient justification for it. How much evidence is required to go from merely having justification for believing something to being justified in believing something? One way to answer this is to imagine that beliefs, like other reports, can be assigned probabilities with respect to their truth. Just as we can ask how probable it is that a newspaper story is true, we can ask the same about a belief. As justification for either sort of report—about the newspaper article or about the belief—accumulates, the probability of its being true increases. Your initial belief in the suspect's guilt might have had only a small probability of being true. But then, as you learn about the fingerprints, the ballistics report, and so on, the probability of the truth of your belief grows. As we have seen, the belief that the suspect killed the victim is either true or not, and whether it is true depends on whether he did in fact kill her. But we can still speak of how *probable* it is that he killed her, given the evidence you have in hand. And for this reason, we might stipulate something like the following: you are justified in believing the suspect is the killer when, given your evidence and reasons, it is more probable that he killed her than that he did not. In other words, a belief evolves from having *some* justification to *being justified* when the available evidence makes the belief's truth more likely than not.

This answer to our question about when a belief becomes justified remains deficient in some obvious respects. Indeed, it seems only to push the question back a step. You are justified in believing something, we are supposing, when the evidence makes its truth more probable than not. But how do we know when this occurs? At what point does the evidence make it more likely than not that the suspect killed the victim? Here opinions may differ. Some people might think that the ballistics report alone tips the scales in favor of his guilt. Others will demand additional evidence, refusing to accept his guilt unless convincing eyewitness testimony supplements the ballistics report. Unfortunately, in most contexts, there exists no sure recipe for determining whether a certain piece of evidence pushes the probability of a belief's truth to over 50 percent. However, given that our concern is with understanding and alleviating the bad thinking that runs rampant in the world today, we do not need such a recipe. No reasonable person, aware of the easily available evidence, should doubt the benefits of vaccines, the fact of global warming, the tragedy of Sandy Hook, the birthplace of Barack Obama, and so on.

Returning, now, to the difference between justified belief and knowledge, remember that a claim to know something is stronger than a claim to be justified in believing something. It is one thing to have a justified belief that the suspect is the murderer, and another thing entirely to know it. The suggestion above—that you are justified in holding a belief when the evidence makes it more likely to be true than not—might tempt you to think that knowledge is nothing but a belief that is *very* highly justified. If, for instance, having a justified belief that the suspect is the murderer requires evidence that makes the belief more likely to be true than not (that is, the chance of its truth is greater than 50 percent), then perhaps *knowing* that he is the murderer requires having a belief that, given the evidence, is something like 90 percent probably true, or 99 percent probably true. But at least since Socrates, philosophers have insisted that justified belief and knowledge differ in a way that cannot be defined purely in terms of the amount of justification available for the belief. Knowing something requires more than possessing a tremendous amount of justification.

The crucial insight rests on our recognition that some justified beliefs might be false, just as some unjustified beliefs might be true. In the second case, when you lack justification for believing something that happens to be true, we should want to deny that you have knowledge. When the victim's sister hears from her clairvoyant acquaintance that the suspect's nemesis is the murderer, she cannot claim to know that he is the murderer, even if it is true that he is. The justification coming from the clairvoyant is no better evidence of the nemesis's guilt than a simple guess, or a coin flip, or a baseless hunch. Justification, then, must play some role in legitimating claims to knowledge. On the other hand, as a result of the nemesis's ingenious but sinister plotting, there is ample evidence that the suspect killed the victim, although he did not. You are quite justified in believing that the original suspect is the perpetrator, but you do not *know* that he is, because the belief is false. Thus, justification cannot be the *only* consideration in claims to knowledge.

What, then, other than justification, is necessary for knowledge? The standard philosophical conception of knowledge demands not only that a belief be justified but that it also be true. You, the detective in charge of the investigation, have been tricked by the suspect's nemesis. As a result of his conniving, you have a justified belief that the suspect is the killer, but you do not know that he is, because your belief is false. To know something requires both that the belief is justified *and* that it is true. No matter how much justification you have, you cannot know something that is false. Knowledge, in short, is a justified *true* belief.[14]

It may seem odd that you cannot know something that is false (although, of course, you can know *that* something is false). However, this requirement simply places knowledge in the company of other things that require the world to be a certain way. You cannot *see* a dragon in the distance because dragons do not exist. At best, you can only think that you see a dragon. Similarly, you cannot be *aware* of the buzzing noise if there is no buzzing noise. Knowledge works the same way. The antivaccination activist can never know that vaccines are harmful, no matter how much justification for her belief she has, if vaccines are not, in fact, harmful. Likewise, regardless of how much evidence the birther collects to justify his belief that President Obama is not a US citizen, he can never know that he is not, given that Obama is indeed a citizen. In the twelfth century, people were justified—given the celestial observations they had at hand and the fact that Galileo's discoveries by means of the telescope were centuries in the future—in believing that the sun revolved around the earth. And prior to Einstein's discovery of the theory of relativity, physicists thought that they knew that the universe operated on Newtonian principles. Newton's physics, after all, was the most justified scientific theory of its day. However, once Einstein replaced it with a different theory, it turned out that these earlier physicists were wrong. What the medievals and the Newtonians "knew" about the workings of the universe they did not know after all. And should future discoveries reveal that Einstein was wrong, it will turn out that no one, ever, *knew* the theory of relativity to be true.

Epistemic Stubbornness, Again

We have now introduced the idea of epistemic stubbornness and considered in broad strokes some important philosophical concepts that clarify what it means for a belief to be justified. Epistemically stubborn people are not, as the article from Patch asserts, dumb. Rather, they are failing to reason in ways that satisfy the standards of sound rational inquiry. They might have some justification for their beliefs, but their beliefs are not sufficiently justified. Epistemically speaking, they ought not to believe what they do. Moreover, they have justification for the correct beliefs, but they fail to give it due credit. Again, epistemically speaking, they ought to believe what they do not. Furthermore, when epistemically stubborn people choose to adopt beliefs that potentially bring harm to others, they are also guilty of a moral failing. Morally speaking, they ought not to believe what they do.

We will now turn from these somewhat abstract ideas concerning evidence, justification, truth, and knowledge to a more concrete discussion of how to reason responsibly. It is one thing to understand, as a purely conceptual matter, the difference between justified and unjustified beliefs, and quite another to develop facility with rules of reasoning that will help you to avoid unjustified beliefs and steer you toward the justified ones.

Chapter 2

How to Be Reasonable

The second chapter of Arthur Conan Doyle's novel *A Study in Scarlet* is titled "The Science of Deduction." The renowned detective Sherlock Holmes explains to Dr. Watson how he knew upon their first encounter that Watson had recently returned from Afghanistan. Applying his "rules of deduction," Holmes reasons as follows: "Here is a gentleman of a medical type, but with the air of a military man. Clearly an army doctor, then. He has just come from the tropics, for his face is dark, and that is not the natural tint of his skin, for his wrists are fair. He has undergone hardship and sickness, as his haggard face says clearly. His left arm has been injured. He holds it in a stiff and unnatural manner. Where in the tropics could an English army doctor have seen much hardship and got his arm wounded? Clearly in Afghanistan."[1] Other instances of Holmes's powers of deduction are sprinkled throughout Doyle's novels and short stories. Looking at another example will help to illuminate a fundamental distinction between two ways that a conclusion might be justified.

The short story "Silver Blaze" finds Holmes and Watson boarding a train to King's Pyland, where the astute detective hopes to solve a case involving a missing racehorse and a murdered trainer.[2] The horse Silver Blaze has mysteriously disappeared from its stable and, had it simply been wandering the moor, would surely have been noticed by one of the many men searching for it. Recognizing that horses have a "gregarious" nature, Holmes suspects that, if not captive, it would try to return home to King's Pyland, where it could enjoy the company of other horses. Alternatively, it might have set off for another stable in Mapleton. Holmes then justifies a decision about where to look for the lost horse with this piece of reasoning: "I have already said that he must have gone to King's Pyland or to Mapleton. He is not at King's Pyland. Therefore, he is at Mapleton."

In both of these examples we have a conclusion—Watson had recently been in Afghanistan, and Silver Blaze, the missing racehorse, is in Mapleton—and a justification for the conclusion. As we have seen, a "justification" consists in reasons or evidence that offer support for some belief. Reasons or evidence increase the probability that a conclusion is true. But how exactly does this work? In what ways might a conclusion be justified?

This question differs from those in the previous chapter, where our concern was to clarify what, broadly speaking, justification is and why a proper respect for justification is our best hope against the kind of bad thinking that marks epistemic stubbornness. The task now is to examine some basic kinds of reasoning that philosophers have developed, some of which trace back thousands of years, at least to Aristotle, whereas others are quite recent, having emerged through philosophical efforts to put scientific reasoning on a firm footing. These reasoning patterns show us how to justify a belief. If you apply these patterns to your own reasoning, you can ensure, or at any rate maximize, the chances that your beliefs are justified. There are also a number of common fallacies to which epistemically stubborn individuals appear especially prone. No one reasons perfectly all the time, philosophers included. However, familiarity with what good and bad reasoning look like is an important first step in combating bad thinking.

Let us return to the two examples of Sherlock Holmes's reasoning. Interestingly, the first example in which Holmes uses his "rules of deduction" in order to identify Watson's recent whereabouts is not, strictly speaking, an instance of deductive reasoning at all. The other example, however, is. How does the nondeductive reasoning in the first case differ from the reasoning on display in the second? What makes some reasoning deductive and some not?

The short answer to the question is this: when done correctly, deductive reasoning—the subject of this chapter—*guarantees* that a conclusion is true if the premises on which it relies are true. For any other type of reasoning—any sort of nondeductive reasoning—this fact does not hold. Only deductive reasoning guarantees you a true conclusion when the premises you are using to support the conclusion are true. By contrast, in any instance of nondeductive reasoning, true premises are not enough to guarantee you a true conclusion; at best, the truth of the premises makes your conclusion *probably* true. That a style of reasoning can guarantee truth makes it a very powerful means by which to justify a belief. Anyone who, when confronted with a legitimately deductive argument, denies its conclusion while agreeing with the premises has made a mistake. Such a person is epistemically at fault. He is not, epistemically speaking, reasoning as he ought to. As for nondeductive reasoning—some forms of which we will examine in the next chapter—while it is not as reliable as deductive reasoning, it nonetheless offers benefits that deduction does not.

In Good Form

Related to the idea of deductive reasoning are concepts like validity and soundness. Clarifying the meaning of these terms is important for understanding how deduction works. To see just how distant from ordinary usage terms like 'validity' are for the philosopher, consider this argument:

1) If Σωκράτης εστιν ανθρωπος, then Σωκράτης εστι βρότος.
2) Σωκράτης εστι βρότος.
3) Therefore, Σωκράτης εστιν ανθρωπος.

Calling this an "argument" means nothing more than that it is a collection of sentences, where the first two are offered in support of, as justification for, the third. The word 'Therefore' that appears in the third sentence is a tip-off that what follows is a conclusion and thus what precedes it are premises. But is the argument deductively valid? Your first thought when hearing this question might be, "How should I know? It's (mostly) Greek to me!" However, a philosopher who looks at this argument—even a philosopher who has no knowledge of Greek—would have no difficulty determining whether the argument is valid.

Validity is a *formal* property of arguments—or, more precisely, a property of the form of a deductive argument. We might capture the idea of an argument's having a particular form by analogy to other linguistic items that are defined in terms of their forms. A haiku, for instance, is a poem that can be identified by its form: it must be three lines long, with the first line containing five syllables, the second line seven, and the third line five again. Notice that with these instructions in hand you could pick out a haiku without knowing anything about the meanings of the words that it contains (although you would have to know how many syllables each word contains). Likewise, once you know that a limerick is five lines long, with a very specific rhyming scheme, you can identify particular poems as limericks even if you have no idea what the limerick is about. The significant point is that haikus and limericks are defined by their form rather than by the content or meaning of the words they contain.

This idea that arguments, like poems, might be analyzed in terms of their form is what makes it possible to look at the argument above, which happens to be about Socrates, and decide whether it is deductively valid even though you may not know a single word of Greek. Just as haikus and limericks must observe certain formal rules in their construction, so, too, must valid arguments. If the argument above satisfies the rules that make an argument valid, then it is valid regardless of what it is about—that is, regardless of what the words in the argument mean. Similarly, if it fails to satisfy the rules of validity, then it is invalid; it is not genuinely deductive. What then are the rules that valid forms of argument must obey?

Before answering this question, let us return to the idea that deductive arguments have particular forms. Think again about the rule that defines a haiku. We have already seen a simple description of this rule: a haiku must be three lines long, with the first line containing five syllables, the second . . . and so on. But we might also have said simply that anything with the following form is a haiku:

Blah blah blah blah blah
Blah blah blah blah blah blah blah
Blah blah blah blah blah

In order to avoid confusion, we might clarify that the 'blah's in the haiku-form are simply stand-ins for syllables. They are like blanks that can be filled in by any syllables at all, one for each 'blah,' and once you do that, you are the proud creator of a haiku.

We can now apply this idea to deductive arguments. The application will require some modifications, given that deductive arguments are not defined in terms of the number and arrangement of syllables that they contain. What *will* matter in isolating the form of an argument is that some strings of words in the argument appear in more than one premise. We must be sure when describing the argument's form to preserve this feature. Here again is the argument presented above:

1) If Σωκράτης εστιν ανθρωπος, then Σωκράτης εστι βρότος.
2) Σωκράτης εστι βρότος.
3) Therefore, Σωκράτης εστιν ανθρωπος.

Notice that in the first premise we have the word 'If' followed by a string of words, and then the word 'then' followed by a different string of words (the strings differ even if they contain some of the same words). The second premise repeats the words that follow 'then' in the first premise. Finally, the conclusion contains the word 'Therefore,' followed by the words that follow the 'If' in the first premise. With these observations in hand we are prepared to exhibit the form of the argument:

1) If A, then B.
2) B.
3) Therefore, A.

Just like the 'blah's in the haiku that can stand for all sorts of syllables, the 'A' and 'B' can stand for any distinct strings of words, as long as those strings form declarative sentences. In the present case 'A' stands for Σωκράτης εστιν ανθρωπος, and

'B' stands for Σωκράτης εστι βρότος. However, we can construct an argument with the *same* form but substituting for 'A' and 'B' different strings of words, like so:

1) If Janet likes to watch horror movies, then she is brave.
2) Janet is brave.
3) Therefore, Janet likes to watch horror movies.

Because this second argument has the same form as the first, and because whether an argument is valid depends simply on its form, we can say that if one of these arguments is valid, then so is the other; if one is invalid, then so, too, is the other.

As we have seen, unlike with haikus, you do not need to think about numbers of syllables when identifying the form of deductive arguments. The strings of words that appear in the premises and conclusion of such arguments can have any number of syllables at all. Another difference is this: whereas haikus all have the *same* form, deductive arguments can have *many* forms. This fact introduces a number of questions. Perhaps the most basic question is one that we have so far only briefly touched on: If deductive arguments can have many forms, then what makes some arguments deductive and some not? What makes Holmes's argument about where to find Silver Blaze deductive but his argument about where Watson came from nondeductive? The next question then takes us back to the issue of validity. If a valid deductive argument is guaranteed to have a true conclusion when it has true premises, then how do we know, given that deductive arguments might possess many different forms, which of these forms are valid and which not? Which arguments are *valid* deductive arguments and which are not?

The answer to the first question cannot be separated from the answer to the second. Deductive arguments are in fact simply those arguments that satisfy the rules of validity. All formally valid arguments are deductive.[3] On the other hand, some arguments might, on their surface, appear to be deductive but are not. Even if their premises are true, their conclusions do not follow from their premises. We might describe arguments that give the appearance of being deductive but are actually not as "formally invalid." This captures the idea that just as deductive arguments are valid in virtue of their form, so, too, some deductive-seeming arguments are invalid (and therefore not truly deductive) in virtue of their form.

An example of this is the argument above about Janet. It certainly looks like a deductive argument. But even if we stipulate that the premises are true, and even if the conclusion *is* true, the conclusion does not follow from those premises—which means that, for all we know (that is, given those premises), the conclusion might be false. This is because the first premise of the argument tells us only that *if* Janet likes to watch horror movies, then she is brave. We do not yet know whether Janet does like to watch horror movies. Then the second premise tells us only that Janet is brave. However, plenty of brave people may not like horror movies. People can be brave for all sorts of reasons having nothing to do with their movie-watching tendencies. Perhaps Janet served valiantly in a war. Thus, the first two premises can be true and the conclusion still false. It could be true that *if* she likes horror movies she is brave; and it could be true that she *is* brave; but it might be false that she likes horror movies. And even if she does happen to like horror movies, that true conclusion does not follow from the truth of the premises.

Because arguments have distinctive forms, we can see even more easily why the argument about Janet is invalid by considering a different argument with the same form:

1) If Janet is a mathematician, then Janet knows that
   $2 + 2 = 4$.
2) Janet knows that $2 + 2 = 4$.
3) Therefore, Janet is a mathematician.

As with the other argument about Janet, we can stipulate that the premises in this argument are true. But the argument is not valid. It is possible, even granting the truth of the premises, that Janet is not a mathematician. If you doubt this, replace Janet's name with *your* name (assuming that you are not a mathematician). Just as many people know that $2 + 2 = 4$ without being mathematicians, many people are brave despite not liking horror moves.

It is now also evident that the argument containing the Greek phrases must be invalid and so is not actually deductive after all. You can know this even if you do not understand Greek because the form of the argument is identical to the invalid form of argument involving Janet. Here, in English, is the argument about Socrates.

1) If Socrates is human, then Socrates is mortal.
2) Socrates is mortal.
3) Therefore, Socrates is human.

Notice that this argument, although invalid, has both true premises and a true conclusion. This reinforces that important point about formally invalid arguments: they might indeed have true conclusions and also true premises. What makes them invalid is not that they lead to false conclusions, but that the premises do not *justify* the conclusion—the conclusion does not follow from the given premises. (As we shall see, not only can invalid arguments have true conclusions, but valid arguments can have false conclusions. What makes an argument valid is not that it leads to a true conclusion, but that the premises justify the conclusion, even if the conclusion is false.)

We have seen that some arguments are formally invalid and so not genuinely deductive. What then distinguishes these formally invalid arguments from other kinds of nondeductive arguments? Perhaps the best answer to this question is simply that formally invalid arguments are those designed with a particular intention in mind: that the conclusion *should* be true in virtue of the argument's form alone. The designer of a formally invalid argument intends to construct a proper deductive argument but fails. The person who wishes to establish Janet's bravery with the argument above *intends* the form of the argument alone to guarantee the truth of the conclusion, even though it does not. In contrast, when Holmes concludes that Watson had served in Afghanistan, his argument does not seem to depend on its formal properties at all; and, despite his exasperating confidence, even Holmes would have to admit the possibility that, even if his assumptions are true, his conclusion might be false. Facts about Watson's bearing, the color of his skin, the angle at which he holds his arm, and so on do not make it impossible for him to have come from somewhere other than Afghanistan. He might have come from India. He might have been vacationing in the British West Indies. Perhaps Watson had colored his skin and held himself with a certain posture in order to deceive Holmes. The great detective himself, after all, often relied on costumes and makeup to mislead others about his true identity. His conclusion about Watson could, for similar or other reasons, be mistaken.

On the other hand, Holmes's reasoning about Silver Blaze's location *does* seem to have the intention characteristic of deductive arguments—establishing a conclusion with absolute certainty by virtue of the form of the argument alone. The argument was this:

1) The horse is at King's Pyland or the horse is at Mapleton.
2) The horse is not at King's Pyland.
3) Therefore, the horse is at Mapleton.

The fact that it is easy to represent the argument in a manner that suggests a particular form (Either A is true or B is true, A is not true, therefore B is true), and that the conclusion is intended to follow from the premises with absolute certainty—that it could not possibly be false if the premises are true—all suggest that Holmes takes himself to be offering a deductive argument.

Deductive arguments, then, are those that offer justification for a conclusion that guarantees its truth. And a deductive argument does this in virtue of having a particular form—a valid form. However, as we have seen, not every form of argument is valid, and so not every argument that *appears* to be deductive guarantees the truth of its conclusion. This is why familiarity with valid forms of argument is so important and an ability to recognize invalid forms—fallacious arguments—is also imperative. If you want to be able to identify bad formal thinking in others, or want to safeguard yourself from engaging in bad formal thinking, you need to be able to distinguish valid argument forms from invalid ones.

How to Make a Valid Argument

Logicians—primarily, philosophers who specialize in logic—have spent considerable time establishing which argument forms are valid and which not. What it all comes down to is not so different from the ideas you learn in a high school geometry class, where you begin with indisputable truths called "axioms" and derive from these axioms other truths, called "theorems." Because the theorems follow from the axioms by rules that preserve truth, they must also be true. In a similar way, logicians can demonstrate for any particular argument form whether it is valid.

The results of these logicians' efforts is a catalog of valid argument forms. These are known as "rules of inference," and each has an identifying label. There is no limit to the number of forms that valid arguments can take, but the rules of inference are especially useful, in part because their validity is fairly easy to see. Using these rules of inference, you can move from premises to a conclusion while remaining certain of the validity of the argument. Once you are familiar with which forms of argument are valid, it becomes a straightforward matter to evaluate any particular form of argument for validity. If the argument takes the form of a valid argument—if it is an instance of a particular rule of inference—it is valid; otherwise, not.

Holmes's argument about where to look for Silver Blaze exemplifies a valid form of argument, one that logicians call "disjunctive syllogism." The disjunctive syllogism form, which we saw above, is this:

1) Either A or B.
2) Not A.
3) Therefore, B.

Because this form is valid, any sentences at all can be "plugged" into 'A' and 'B,' and the result will be a valid argument. Thus, the following are both valid:

1) Either the king ate the cake or the queen ate the cake.
2) The king did not eat the cake.
3) Therefore, the queen ate the cake.

And,

1) Either the house burned down or the police arrested the arsonist.
2) The house did not burn down.
3) Therefore, the police arrested the arsonist.

Because these two arguments have the form of a disjunctive syllogism, and because disjunctive syllogism is a valid *form* of argument, we know that these are both valid arguments. That is, we know with certainty that if the premises in the arguments are true, their conclusions must be true as well. In fact, most people tacitly use the disjunctive syllogism every day of their lives without thinking about it:

1) The jam is either in the cupboard or it is in the fridge.
2) The jam is not in the cupboard.
3) Therefore, the jam is in the fridge.

Still another valid argument form is called *modus ponens*, which translates loosely from Latin to mean "method of affirming." Here is its form:

1) If A, then B.
2) A.
3) Therefore, B.

This form looks similar to the one we saw when examining the arguments about Socrates and Janet. The form of those arguments, however, we now know, was invalid. The description of that invalid form of argument is "the fallacy of affirming the consequent." This appellation makes sense because in a sentence of the form "If A then B," usually called a "conditional statement," the sentence replacing 'A' is called the "antecedent," and that which replaces 'B' is the "consequent." So, when committing the fallacy of affirming the consequent, you are making the mistake of concluding that the antecedent of a conditional statement is true because the consequent is true. In the case of Janet, on the basis of the conditional statement that "If Janet likes to watch horror movies, then Janet is brave," we concluded that Janet liked to watch horror movies (the antecedent of the conditional) only because we affirmed that Janet is brave (which is the consequent of the conditional). In fact, in a valid argument it is the other way around: as the *modus ponens* form of argument illustrates, if the antecedent of a conditional statement is true then so is the consequent.

Moreover, just as was the case with disjunctive syllogism, once you know that *modus ponens* is a valid form of argument, you know as well that any argument that has that form is valid. Thus, the following argument must be valid:

1) If mosquitoes have six legs, then mosquitoes are insects.
2) Mosquitoes have six legs.
3) Therefore, mosquitoes are insects.

And:

1) If Venus is a planet, then unicorns exist.
2) Venus is a planet.
3) Therefore, unicorns exist.

Perhaps you are surprised to learn that this last argument is valid given that its conclusion is undeniably false. But this reaction misses the point of validity. Validity, remember, is about the *form* an argument has and not about what the sentences in the argument mean. To deny the validity of an argument because it has a false conclusion is like denying that a poem is a haiku because it is silly, upsetting, trite or even totally incomprehensible nonsense. What makes a poem a haiku is just its form; likewise, what makes a deductive argument valid is just its form.

But what good is validity if valid arguments might have false conclusions? The discovery of valid argument forms deserves its place as one of humankind's greatest intellectual achievements. This is because, first of all, it allows you to detect instances of *in*validity—that is, fallacies in reasoning—and this is no mean achievement. Our primary purpose in this book is to identify (and, we hope, provide remedies for) various kinds of bad thinking, and logically fallacious reasoning is right there at the top of the list.

Moreover, access to the valid forms of reasoning provides us with a surefire recipe for deducing true conclusions from *true* premises. If the premises of an argument are *not* true, as happens to be the case with the first premise in the argument about unicorns, then validity cannot work its magic on the conclusion. A valid argument form all on its own cannot make a conclusion true. For that it needs help from its premises. But if the premises do their job—if they say something true—then the valid argument form can do the rest. It can guarantee a true conclusion.

This is remarkable when you think about it. Holmes's first argument about where Watson had recently been living is not valid. All of the premises, even if true, do not make it impossible that Watson had arrived in London from somewhere other than Afghanistan. On the other hand, Holmes's second argument, assuming that its premises are true, *does* provide certainty about the conclusion: Silver Blaze *must* be in Mapleton. Given that Holmes's reasoning has the form of a disjunctive syllogism and that the premises in the argument are true, it is literally impossible that Silver Blaze is anywhere but Mapleton.

As the unicorn example makes clear, some valid arguments have true premises and some do not. When a philosopher describes an argument as "sound," she is making a stronger claim than when she describes it as valid. A "sound" argument, in the philosopher's technical sense of the term, is a valid argument with true premises. Thus, a sound argument, unlike the valid unicorn argument (which contains a false premise) or the invalid Janet argument (which may have true premises and a true conclusion but nonetheless commits the fallacy of affirming the consequent), *must* have a true conclusion. So, when reasoning deductively, it is to sound arguments that philosophers—indeed, everyone—should aspire.

Begging the Question

The above advice does come with an important caveat, however—one to which any discussion of bad thinking must attend. Among the most common mistakes of bad thinkers is a fallacy known as "begging the question." The expression itself, unfortunately, is a source of confusion. You might hear it frequently misused, as in contexts like these: "the growing demand for gasoline begs the question whether prices will increase," or "the tennis player's injury begs the question whether she will make it to the finals." In these examples, the phrase 'begging the question' simply means "raises the question." But this is not, strictly speaking, the actual meaning of the phrase. To be fair, that actual meaning is also not very well characterized as begging the question. It turns out that 'begging the question' is a phrase that arose from a mistranslation of a Latin expression around five hundred years ago—*petitio principii*—which in turn was a mistranslation of a Greek phrase that Aristotle introduced almost two thousand years before that.

To understand the kind of bad thinking that begging the question involves, suppose you are unsure of whether Madagascar is an island, and so you ask a friend. Your friend believes that Madagascar is an island and offers you this argument in an effort to convince you:

1) Madagascar is an island.
2) Therefore, Madagascar is an island.

This argument is very clearly defective in some respect, but it cannot be criticized for being invalid. It is valid! If the premise is true, then the conclusion must be true as well—how could it not be, given that it says the same thing as the premise? Moreover, the argument is sound. We know this because the premise is true: Madagascar is an island. Thus, we have a valid argument with a true premise, which is just the definition of soundness.

The defect in the argument is not that it fails to be sound, but rather that no one who doubts the conclusion of the argument would be willing to accept the premise. If the premise of an argument says the same thing as the conclusion, then the argument will never succeed in convincing someone of a conclusion that he or she is not already willing to accept. In the present case, if you refuse to believe that Madagascar is an island, or are merely unsure whether it is an island, you will also deny or be skeptical of the premise that says it is an island. The reasoning is circular: you will not accept the premise, A, unless you already believe the conclusion, B; but you cannot believe B without accepting A.

Of course, the defect in the argument about Madagascar is tremendously easy to spot because the premise and conclusion are literally identical. But suppose that your friend had argued like this:

1) Madagascar is surrounded on all sides by water.
2) Therefore, Madagascar is an island.

This argument, too, begs the question, although a bit more subtly than the previous one.[4] To see this, imagine once more that you, who know perfectly well what the definition of an island is, doubt that Madagascar is an island, and so are hoping to hear from your friend compelling reasons to believe that it is. But if you doubt that Madagascar is an island, then you should also doubt that Madagascar is surrounded on all sides by water, because that is just what it means to be an island. Your friend's argument begs the question. The argument is sound but nevertheless unpersuasive because no one who doubts the conclusion would accept the premise.

Once you become attuned to the kind of bad thinking inherent in the fallacy of begging the question, you begin to see instances of it everywhere. A classic example of an argument that begs the question is this:

1) The words of the Bible are divinely inspired, and they proclaim that God exists.
2) Therefore, God exists.

If you put yourselves into the shoes of someone who doubts God's existence, presumably the target audience for this argument, then the bad thinking inherent in this reasoning becomes instantly apparent. Why, if you doubt God's existence, would you accept the claim that the words of the Bible are divinely inspired? Only those who accept the conclusion of the argument can accept the premise. The argument is valid (we will not comment on whether it is sound), but still no good.

Or, to take another, somewhat different kind of example, suppose you attend a debate between political opponents, one of whom attacks the other for being a socialist. Why is socialism bad? The critic offers this:

1) Any political system that puts the means of production into the hands of the community or government is bad.
2) Therefore, socialism is bad.

Despite the validity of this argument (again, we offer no comment on its soundness), it could hardly convince a socialist to abandon his or her political commitments. Socialism just is a form of political system that puts the means of production into the hands of the community or government, and so a socialist would never accept the premise in this argument. Only someone who already believed that the conclusion is true would endorse the premise, which is just to say that the argument begs the question.

Vaccines cause autism, therefore they are harmful. Human activities cannot cause global warming because nothing anyone does can cause the climate to change. The COVID-19 pandemic is a hoax because the medical "experts" the government relies on are making it all up. Arguments like these—all too common on the Internet and, more gravely, in interviews that enjoy the appearance of respectability because they appear in mainstream media—beg the question. They may be valid (and, in these cases, we are happy to comment on their soundness—they are not!), but for reasons that you should now be able to identify, they are defective nevertheless.

Why Care about Deductive Reasoning?

In closing this discussion of deductive reasoning, we want to consider its relevance to our goal of alleviating the bad thinking that we see harming America—and the world at large—today.

What good is a primer on good thinking if, as seems to be the case, recognizing and constructing deductive arguments requires special knowledge of valid argument forms—knowledge that might not be so easy to attain or apply? To be sure, this is a legitimate concern. However, knowing some basic features of deductive arguments remains valuable for several reasons. First, even if you cannot always be certain that an argument or justification you are offering for a position is valid, the idea that deductive arguments should be assessed in terms of validity remains powerful. Anyone—whether you or an interlocutor— who argues in a deductive fashion incurs a rather heavy burden. The price of trying to argue that your conclusion cannot possibly be false is that you must play by some very strict rules. It is fair game to challenge any apparently deductive argument if you suspect it of violating these rules.

Second, it is all too common in discussions about important issues like whether the earth is warming, or vaccines are safe, or 5G networks facilitate the spread of COVID-19, for people to issue disclaimers that one side or the other is "free" to have its own opinions, as if this should suffice to end the dispute. Yet, although opinions might differ with respect to the truth of particular premises in a deductive argument, differences of opinion concerning the validity of an argument should not be tolerated. Whether an argument is valid is an objective matter of (logical) fact—it is as impervious to subjective opinion as whether a square has four sides. This should bring a refreshing level of rigor to debates. It means requiring of anyone who offers a deductive argument that they be able to defend its validity if challenged. When it comes to the validity of deductive arguments, "agree to disagree" is no longer on the table.

Finally, because deductively valid arguments offer the strongest possible justification for a belief, adhering to the strict guidelines that determine validity may be worth the effort. If you can produce an argument for your position that is demonstratively both valid and contains only true premises (and thus is also sound), you can and need do no more in support of your conclusion. On the other hand, if in trying to produce such an argument you see no route to success, you have still learned something important. You have discovered that the conclusion you aim to justify might possibly be false. But this discovery does not require you to abandon your position. Rather, it suggests only that you need to find some other way to justify your conclusion, one that may not make that conclusion absolutely certain but that might nevertheless make it at least very probable.

This brings us to another canonical form of reasoning, one that, while less certain in its conclusions than deductive reasoning, is usually the best we can do. It is the reasoning that you used in the previous chapter when playing detective, that Sherlock Holmes employs to determine just where his colleague Watson has been, that scientists use when justifying their hypotheses, and that we lay people typically rely on every day to make sense of the world around us.

Chapter 3

Thinking and Explaining

How much easier life would be if we could rely on deductive reasoning to justify all of our beliefs. Because logicians have developed objective means by which to evaluate arguments for validity, anytime someone defended a conclusion, we could put their reasoning to the test to see whether it conforms to rules of validity. The conclusions of valid reasoning might still be false, because the premises involved might be false. But if we focus only on the question of whether a conclusion is *justified* by some collection of premises, nothing beats validity.

Unfortunately, this easy life is not our life. Much of what we believe and know about the world depends not so much on conclusions we deduce from premises but on inferences from observations we make. So far, despite centuries of unrelenting work on inferences of these sorts, philosophers have not been able to devise a foolproof method of assessing them. Nothing comparable to the science of deduction exists for instances of reasoning to which concepts like validity and soundness simply do not apply.

How Certain Are You?

Nondeductive reasoning is any reasoning that cannot be evaluated in terms of validity. The premises of a nondeductive argument, even if true, will not guarantee the truth of a conclusion. A belief you form on the basis of nondeductive reasoning is always at risk of being false. However, this does not mean that such reasoning should not be trusted or that beliefs formed on its basis should always be accepted with a grain of salt. Nondeductive reasoning may not deliver the goods that deduction promises, but the goods it does deliver, when performed correctly, are often good enough.

Indeed, despite its deficiency relative to deductive reasoning, it is nondeductive reasoning that makes life possible. We reason nondeductively all the time, even if we do not recognize the numerous occasions on which we do so. When you drank your coffee this morning you probably believed that it would taste pretty much like it did on every previous day. When you pushed the button to start your car, you naturally assumed that the engine would come to life. And when you returned home from work, you did so with the belief that your house or apartment would still be standing. All of these beliefs are justified, but none of them are absolutely (deductively) certain. Perhaps the coffee you purchased had been burned or the battery in your car had died or a fire had destroyed your domicile. These might be highly unlikely possibilities in the circumstances, but still, they are possible, and so they undermine the absolute certainty of your beliefs.

In an earlier chapter, we contrasted the kind of reasoning that leads to the conclusion that the zoo is open with the reasoning that should have led a person to believe that her spouse was cheating on her. The former reasoning, we now know, was deductive. The second kind of reasoning is nondeductive. The clues available to the spouse—the texts in the middle of the night, the cruise tickets hidden beneath the mattress—justify the belief that her partner is unfaithful. However, they do not make that conclusion absolutely certain. An innocent explanation of the partner's behavior, even if unlikely, is not out of the question.

The role of the detective in search of the victim's murderer, which we also considered in a previous chapter, provides another example of nondeductive reasoning. Initially there was justification for thinking that one suspect was the murderer. That conclusion might have been false, even if well justified. And as additional evidence arrived, we saw the justification shift in favor of a different conclusion. The suspect's nemesis had killed the victim. Still, even that conclusion, no matter how strong the justification, could be wrong. Even if the nemesis confesses, there is some chance, however remote, that believing in his guilt is an error. Maybe he had been brainwashed by some unknown third party. The nemesis thought he was framing the first suspect when in fact he himself had been framed.

The odds of such brainwashing in this case are ridiculously low, but its mere possibility brings out two important ideas relative to the distinction between deductive and nondeductive reasoning. The first is that the kind of certainty provided by sound deductive arguments—those that are valid and contain only true premises—is absolute in a very literal sense. If a sound deductive argument concludes that the nemesis killed the victim, then it should not be possible even to *imagine* circumstances in which the premises are true and he is not the murderer. Second, it is clear why the possibility that nondeductive arguments may lead to false conclusions is not by itself cause for great concern. Sometimes—indeed, often—the possibility that a nondeductively supported conclusion is false is utterly remote. For that reason, nondeductive arguments can be relied on to justify beliefs even if, unlike sound deductive arguments, they leave room for error.

Deductive and nondeductive arguments differ in another way as well. Deductive arguments all proceed in pretty much the same way. Premises are offered, and a conclusion is drawn with the intention that it all matches a valid form of argument. But nondeductive arguments do not typically emulate particular forms. Some involve simply enumerating past instances in which the world has been a certain way and conclude that when circumstances resemble those in the past, the world will again follow suit. For instance, you conclude that the next time you push the ignition button in your car the engine will start because previously, whenever you pushed the button, the engine started. Or you have observed that roughly one in every five dozen eggs you have purchased is broken, and so you conclude that there will be a broken egg in the next five dozen you purchase. Nondeductive reasoning like this is sometimes called "induction by enumeration."

But now consider the detective's justification for believing that the suspect or his nemesis murdered the victim. The reasoning that justifies that conclusion is just like the reasoning that Sherlock Holmes uses to justify his conclusion that Dr. Watson had spent time in Afghanistan. In nondeductive reasoning of this sort, which is sometimes called "abduction," or "inference to the best explanation," a series of facts or observations is collected, and then a hypothesis is offered that would explain these facts or observations. Holmes, for example, makes the following observations:

1) Watson appears to be a doctor.
2) Watson has the carriage of a military type.

3) Watson's face is dark but his wrists are pale, suggesting that he has been exposed to the sun, and so he has been living in a tropical climate.
4) Watson's face is haggard, suggesting he has suffered hardship.
5) Watson's left arm is held at an awkward angle, suggesting that he has been injured.

Having accumulated these observations, the next step in reasoning is to offer a hypothesis or explanation that would tie them all together—that would make sense of them all. If Watson had served in Afghanistan, then you would expect the observations to which Holmes draws our attention. The conclusion that Watson had been in Afghanistan is justified because it explains all the observations. And notice too that in this example of inference to the best explanation, some of the observations on which Holmes relies are themselves conclusions of just this sort of reasoning. For instance, the third observation, that Watson had been living in a tropical locale, is a conclusion drawn from the observations that his face is dark but his wrists pale; and the fourth observation, that Watson had faced hardship, is an inference that explains why his face appears haggard.

Just as induction by enumeration can justify a conclusion without making the conclusion absolutely certain—the car may not start the next time you press the ignition button, and there may be two or zero broken eggs in the next five cartons you buy—so, too, inference to the best explanation is fallible. Watson's haggard face might be the result of a strained marriage rather than war-related trauma. His complexion is consistent with having been in Afghanistan, but other sunny locales would have darkened his skin just the same.

For both sorts of nondeductive reasoning, more is better. When relying on enumeration to justify a belief, the larger the sample of things that you have observed, the more confidence you should have about the properties of things outside your sample. Your belief that one in the next sixty eggs that you purchase will be broken is more justified if it is based on having purchased three thousand, rather than three hundred, eggs. And the more observations that can be explained by assuming that the nemesis had murdered the victim, or that Watson had lived in Afghanistan, the more likely it is that the nemesis did in fact murder the victim and that Watson did indeed live in Afghanistan.

Nondeductive reasoning, in either its inductive or abductive form, is far more pervasive than deductive reasoning. Much of what we believe is justified either on the basis of past experience, which involves enumerative induction, or on the basis of "what makes the most sense" of what we observe, which depends on inference to the best explanation. However, accompanying each sort of reasoning are traps that must be avoided.

Small Samples and False Patterns

Difficulties involving induction by enumeration are easier to identify. Enumerative induction is essentially a process in which you rely on what you know about a sample—a collection of things—in order to justify a belief about things outside the sample. The number of cups of coffee you have enjoyed in your lifetime is a sample that can be used to justify your belief about the taste of the next cup you drink. Similarly, the number of occasions on which you have started your car with a press of a button is a sample that justifies your belief about what will happen the next time you press the button. Because you have bought hundreds of dozens of eggs in your lifetime, you are justified in believing that one in every five dozen will be broken. But reasoning from a sample of things to other things outside the sample comes with risk. One obvious concern is whether the sample is large enough to justify a belief about something outside the sample. If you have had only one cup of coffee in your life and it tasted bitter, the justification for believing that the next cup will also taste bitter is much weaker than had you drunk ten cups or a hundred cups. When the sample on which you are relying is too small, there is a chance that its members do not behave in a way that is representative of a larger class. Small samples tend to exhibit extremes that are not present in larger samples, tempting one to see patterns where none in fact exist. To see how this temptation leads to bad thinking, it is worth considering a real-life example in which a belief based on small samples caused a number of charitable foundations to misdirect hundreds of millions of dollars.

Suppose you are wondering whether your child would be better off in the small high school in a nearby town or in the local large high school. Your main concern is with academic achievement. You want your child to attend the school where her chance of academic success is greatest, and if that means moving to the nearby town where your child can enroll in the smaller high school, you are willing to do so. In order to justify your belief about whether small high schools perform better than large ones, you find some studies that show a correlation between small school size and high levels of academic achievement. As you continue to read up on the issue, you find that you share your growing confidence in the superiority of small high schools with some elite company. The Bill and Melinda Gates Foundation has spent close to two billion dollars on efforts to improve education, with a lot of this money earmarked for converting large schools into groups of smaller ones. Prestigious donors, such as the Annenberg Foundation and the Carnegie Foundation, jumped on board the small-schools initiative.

Justifying the actions of these organizations were data that show small schools to be overrepresented among schools with high-achieving students. That is, when you look at the schools that are producing the highest proportion of best students—measured by students with the highest scores on standardized tests—a lot more of them are small than you would expect if the size of the school made no difference. This seems like a good reason to put your house on the market and move to the nearby town where your daughter can enroll in the small high school. Small schools must do something different from what large schools do. Whatever it is they do differently, it works. They produce better students.

This is not a fanciful example. The Gates Foundation really did spend close to two billion dollars in order to convert large schools into smaller ones. Foundations like Annenberg and Carnegie also contributed to the effort. However, these good intentions were for naught. The inductive reasoning that had been used to justify the conclusion that small schools outperform large ones was based on an error.[1] Supporters of the small-school initiative failed to consider the importance of sample size when reasoning inductively.

To understand the error, imagine that a friend challenges you to guess whether the coin she is about to flip is fair. She flips it three times, and it comes up heads on each occasion. Three heads in a row is a somewhat surprising result, but not nearly as surprising as ten heads in a row or a hundred heads in a row. With a small sample of flips—only three—you are more likely to see a run of heads than you would, assuming a fair coin, if the coin had been flipped ten or a hundred times. It would be bad thinking to infer on the basis of such a small sample that the coin is biased.

The same point holds when thinking about the performance of students in small schools. Small schools are like small sequences of coin flips. Just as we should not be very surprised to find a sequence of three heads in three coin flips, we should not be shocked to find an unusually high proportion of good students in a small school. A small school is far more likely to have, say, 20 percent of its students in a high-achieving group compared to only 5 percent in a large school. The reason we are more likely to find a higher proportion of excellent students in a smaller school than in a larger school is just the same as the reason we are more likely to encounter only heads when flipping a fair coin three times than when flipping the same coin twenty times. That the proportions of unusual students will vary more in smaller schools than in larger ones also means that some other small schools are more likely to have a higher proportion of *bad* students than a larger school—just as you are more likely to see a run of *tails* in sequences of three coin flips than in sequences of twenty flips, given a fair coin. And this is just what statisticians who have studied the issue have noticed. Not only are small schools overrepresented for having high proportions of excellent students; they are also overrepresented for having high proportions of low-achieving students. In the end, a variety of factors suggests that if the goal for your child is high academic achievement, then the prospects are better in a large school than a small school.[2] Even the Gates Foundation seems to have figured out that the small-school initiative was failing to improve overall student achievement, and it has accordingly shifted its resources in different directions.

There is a second lesson to be drawn from this case.[3] Not only do small sample sizes tempt one to see patterns that do not actually exist—there is no real correlation between small schools and academic performance—but people show an irresistible tendency to offer causal explanations for these faux patterns. Upon learning of the higher proportion of academic standouts in small schools, people jump to the conclusion that smaller schools must do something that explains the higher proportion. Perhaps the schools provide more individualized attention to the students, or they offer a more congenial social environment, or they embrace and celebrate the idiosyncrasies of their students. But these are simply "just so" stories, made up for the purpose of explaining a pattern that in reality has no causal explanation. The real reason that some small schools have a higher proportion of excellent students is simply a consequence of the fact that unusual occurrences, like a run of three heads, are more likely to appear in a small sample. This is why, for the same reason, some small schools have a higher proportion of low-performing students.

The kind of bad thinking that prompted a misguided drive toward smaller schools has obvious analogues in other contexts. Suppose you read about a number of small towns in which the incidence of autism is higher than the national average. It might be tempting to think that something is causing the higher incidence in these towns. Just as the unusually large proportion of high-achieving students in a small school seems to cry out for an explanation, so too might the surprising percentage of children with autism in small towns. You begin to look for an explanation of this pattern. Perhaps vaccines are causing the high rate of autism. But this is bad thinking. The reason that some small towns might be home to a larger-than-average number of children with autism is simply because they are small. Other small towns will have *smaller*-than-average numbers of children afflicted with autism.

To take a similar case, it turns out that there is an unusually low rate of kidney cancer in certain sparsely populated rural counties.[4] This makes a causal explanation enticing. Maybe lakes and streams in rural areas are less polluted and the air is purer. But there is also an unusually *high* rate of kidney cancer in other sparsely populated rural counties. Maybe people in rural areas smoke heavily and have poor diets. These causal explanations are instances of bad thinking. In fact, the low and high rates of cancer that can be observed in rural communities are both simply the effect of small samples. But small samples breed extremes for no reason other than happenstance, which often makes the hunt for causal explanations pointless.

Moreover, as we have seen, when these erroneous explanations then guide actions and policy decisions, they can do momentous harm. They can prevent wise allocations of resources, as in the vast sums that charitable foundations spent to create small schools. They can encourage people to assign blame where it does not belong, leading them to avoid practices like vaccinations that are in fact helpful. Or they might persuade you to uproot your life in search of an unestablished good, as would happen if you chose to move to a rural county in the belief that country living will reduce the risk of cancer. As these examples testify, the bad thinking that rests on extrapolations from small samples can easily lead to adverse outcomes. At the same time, the "fix" is easy. All you need to do is make sure, whenever possible, that your inductive reasoning is based on large enough samples.

Confirmation Bias

So far, we have been examining enumerative inductive reasoning, and we have seen that when seeking to justify a belief on this basis it is important to take care to consider a sufficiently large sample. The other sort of nondeductive reasoning—abduction, or inference to the best explanation—faces vulnerabilities of other sorts. When reasoning abductively you are justifying a belief on the grounds that it does the best job explaining some collection of observations. Watson must have been in Afghanistan because that would explain why he has a haggard face, tanned complexion, and an injured arm. But how do you decide what the best explanation is for some collection of observations? Which observations should you be considering as in need of an explanation in the first place? Although no precise answers to these questions are possible, philosophers, as well as psychologists and statisticians, have offered ideas or made discoveries that can help to prevent careless use of abduction.

First, there is the question about observations. When looking to justify a particular belief on the grounds that it is the best explanation for a series of observations, is there a class or kind of observation that deserves special attention? A clue arrives in the form of a caution from the early modern English philosopher Francis Bacon (1561–1626), who is a principal figure in the development of the scientific method. Bacon writes:

> The human understanding when it has once adopted an opinion (either as being the received opinion or as being agreeable to itself) draws all things else to support and agree with it. And though there be a greater number and weight of instances to be found on the other side, yet these it either neglects and despises, or else by some distinction sets aside and rejects; in order that by this great and pernicious predetermination the authority of its former conclusions may remain inviolate. . . . And such is the way of all superstition, whether in astrology, dreams, omens, divine judgments, or the like; wherein men, having a delight in such vanities, mark the events where they are fulfilled, but where they fail,

though this happen much oftener, neglect and pass them by. . . . [I]t is the peculiar and perpetual error of the human intellect to be more moved and excited by affirmatives than by negatives; whereas it ought properly to hold itself indifferently disposed towards both alike. Indeed in the establishment of any true axiom, the negative instance is the more forcible of the two.[5]

Bacon is decrying the human tendency to give more weight to observations that confirm a preferred belief than to observations that might challenge the belief. This tendency—to favor confirming evidence over disconfirming evidence—has become the subject of a large psychological literature. The kind of bad thinking that Bacon complains about has come to be known as "confirmation bias."

To clarify the nature of confirmation bias and understand the sort of bad thinking it produces, it is helpful to consider a number of experiments carried out by the psychologist P. C. Wason. The first experiment requires you to identify a rule that defines how sequences of three numbers are created. For instance, you might be provided with the sequence 2-4-6.[6] You are then allowed to offer sequences of your own in an attempt to justify your belief about the content of the rule. The experimenter will tell you, for each sequence you suggest, whether it conforms to the rule. Seeing that the initial sequence contains three even numbers, each separated by two, you might suspect that this is the correct description of the rule. Then to test whether you are right you propose the sequences 8-10-12 and 22-24-26. The experimenter reports that each of these sequences conforms to the rule, and, feeling confident, you declare that the rule is in fact that the three numbers in the sequence must be even and separated by two.

On the other hand, perhaps you suspect that the rule simply requires that the numbers in the sequence be separated by two, but not that they must be even. To test whether this is the rule you suggest sequences like 5-7-9 and 8-10-12. The experimenter informs you that your proposed sequences indeed satisfy the rule, and so you assert, again with confidence, that the rule is as you suspected: the numbers in the sequence must be separated by two.

Consider another example that, although on the surface very different from the first experiment, is similar at a deeper level.[7] In this experiment, instead of trying to discover a rule on the basis of samples that you generate, you are trying to test whether a given rule is true. The rule you are asked to evaluate concerns four cards, each of which has a letter on one of its sides and a number on the other. The rule you are asked to evaluate is this: *If a card has a vowel on one side, then it has an even number on the other side.* The cards you see are these:

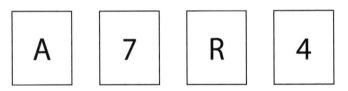

The question seems simple: Which cards must you turn over in order to know whether the rule is true—that is, whether it is true that if a card has a vowel on one side, then it has an even number on the other side. Yet, despite the apparent simplicity of the question, nearly all subjects in this experiment give the wrong answer.

It is important to see the relevance of these experiments to abductive reasoning. Just as Holmes's hypothesis about where Watson had come from was justified on the basis of how well it explained a set of observations, so too the subjects of these experiments are evaluating hypotheses on the basis of how well they account for a collection of observations. In the first experiment, subjects are trying to guess the rule that does the best job "explaining" the sequences of numbers they offer. For instance, the rule "even numbers separated by two" makes sense of the sequences 2-4-6, 8-10-12, and 22-24-26, while the rule "odd numbers separated by four" does not. Therefore, inference to the best explanation guides you to prefer the first rule over the second. Likewise, in the second experiment, you are given the rule and your task is to figure out which observations you must make in order to show that it, rather than some other rule, is true. You are in effect being asked about what you should expect to see on the other sides of the cards if the rule were true.[8]

If you are like most of the subjects in the second experiment, you will have chosen to turn over the card with the A on its front, and perhaps also the card with the 4. Turning over the A-card makes sense: if you discover an odd number on the other side, then you know the rule that cards with vowels on one side have even numbers on the other side is false. It is also clear that you should not turn over the R-card because the rule says nothing about the kind of number (odd or even) that must be opposite a consonant. However, turning over the card with the 4 is a mistake. To see why, suppose that on the other side of the card is a consonant. The rule does not specify that cards with consonants on one side cannot have even numbers on the other, and so you learn nothing about the truth of the rule in this case. But if you find a vowel on the other side, you also do not learn whether the rule is true because, for all you now know, some cards with even numbers on one side have vowels on the other side and some do not. Discovering a vowel on the other side of the 4-card goes toward *confirming* the rule—that is, lends support to the belief that it is true. But the problem is that the discovery still does not preclude the possibility that some cards have vowels on one side and *odd* numbers on the other. You have learned that some cards satisfy the rule, but you have not yet learned whether *all* cards do. Counterintuitively, in order to determine whether the rule is true, you must look for evidence that it is *false*. You must, that is, try to *disconfirm* it. To do this you should flip over the card with the 7 on its front. If a vowel is present on the other side, then you know that the rule is false. The 7-card is diagnostic in a way that the 4-card is not.

The results of these psychological experiments reveal a confirmation bias in their subjects. Rather than looking for evidence that would truly test a hypothesis—in this case, a rule— they would look only for evidence that would confirm it. To test a hypothesis correctly, you must think about the sort of evidence that would show it to be false.[9] If you are wondering, for instance, whether it is true that everyone who is drinking beer at the party is over twenty-one years old, you should check the IDs of the people who look *younger* than twenty-one. You need not bother to check the IDs of people who are obviously older than twenty-one, even though doing so would help to confirm the rule that you must be over twenty-one to drink beer. The same reasoning is true in the card experiment. You must look for violations of the rule in order to know whether it is true, which means that you need to check the card with the odd number on one side to see whether it has a vowel on the other.

The first experiment involving the sequences of numbers makes the same point. If you start with the belief that the rule defining the number sequences is "even numbers separated by two," then when the experimenter confirms for you that the sequences 8-10-12 and 22-24-26 satisfy the rule, you have gained additional evidence that your hypothesis is correct, but you have not actually tested the hypothesis. You can list sequences of even numbers, separated by two, all day long without learning whether you have hit on the intended rule. On the other hand, if you suggest 8-10-11, or 13-17-22, and the experimenter tells you that these sequences also satisfy the rule, then you have learned something. You now know that your hypothesis is false. In fact, the rule that subjects were supposed to discover stated simply that the numbers must appear in ascending order. Subjects would not be able to know this unless they suggested sequences of numbers that did not appear in ascending order—that is, unless they looked for sequences of numbers that would violate the rule.

Wason's experiments were influenced in part by the work of the philosopher Sir Karl Popper (1902–94). Popper was interested in how scientific theories might be distinguished from "pseudoscientific" theories, such as astrology or numerology.[10] He saw in genuinely scientific theories, like Einstein's theory of general relativity, a willingness to take risks. By this Popper meant that scientific theories make predictions that could be either true or *false* about the world. If false, the failed prediction would count as a significant strike against the theory that generated it. Testing a theory, Popper argued, requires looking for ways to show that it is false.

In contrast, the predictions of a pseudoscience like astrology are so vague that they can always be interpreted in ways that make them true. If your astrologer predicts that you will have a great triumph at work today, and you later come home feeling defeated after losing a client or receiving angry complaints from customers, your astrologer might still insist her prediction was correct. You now have the freedom to look for better clients, she tells you, or your customers must care deeply about your services. Consistency-with-every-result is not how science works. For instance, Einstein's theory predicted that starlight should bend a precise amount around massive bodies. This prediction "sticks it neck out" in a way the astrologer's does not. Einstein's prediction, unlike the astrologer's, might have been wrong, and if it were, this would have dealt a serious blow to the theory of general relativity.

Popper's thought that testing for the truth of a belief requires looking for ways to show that it is false is of a piece with the passage from Bacon. Bacon describes in plain words the same temptation to look for evidence that favors a belief and to ignore evidence that tells against it that Wason demonstrated experimentally. We can see more clearly now the wisdom behind Bacon's comment that "it is the peculiar and perpetual error of the human intellect to be more moved and excited by affirmatives than by negatives; whereas it ought properly to hold itself indifferently disposed towards both alike. Indeed in the establishment of any true axiom, the negative instance is the more forcible of the two."

Were conspiracy theorists to embrace Bacon's emphasis on the "negative instance," they might see how their conclusions rest on bad thinking. The confirmation bias is hard at work in conspiracy theories like the idea that the Sandy Hook school shooting was staged for the purpose of tightening gun controls. It also lies behind the antivaccination movement and, even more recently, it is at play in the connection that many people have drawn between the COVID-19 virus outbreak and the increasing use of 5G networks. The typical path a conspiracy theory takes begins with a false claim. In the case of the antivaccination movement, the prestigious medical journal *Lancet* published a paper in 1998 by Dr. Andrew Wakefield. Based on a small sample (and we have seen already why conclusions based on small samples are unreliable), Wakefield claimed that the vaccine for measles, mumps, and rubella caused developmental disorders in children. *Lancet* has since retracted the article, and Wakefield's medical license has been revoked because his conclusions rested on data that, it turned out, he had simply made up, presumably for the purpose of promoting a company he had created that would sell his own replacement vaccines. But by the time *Lancet* retracted the article in 2010, it was too late.

Bacon has once more proved prophetic. He might just as well be describing members of the antivaccination community when he says: "And such is the way of all superstition, whether in astrology, dreams, omens, divine judgments, or the like; wherein men, having a delight in such vanities, mark the events where they are fulfilled, but where they fail, though this happen much oftener, neglect and pass them by." Conspiracy theorists jumped on Wakefield's fraudulent study perhaps because it confirmed their preexisting distrust of government-sponsored health initiatives.[11] Rather than looking for evidence that spoke against the harmfulness of vaccines, they looked only for confirming evidence. So when movie stars like Jenny McCarthy and celebrities like Robert F. Kennedy Jr. rail against vaccines, this seems to the antivaccination community more compelling than the numerous studies published by medical researchers that show vaccines to be harmless.[12] Then, when a Russian disinformation campaign floods the Internet with false stories about the dangers of vaccines, the antivaccination movement again hears what it wants to hear. If members of the antivaccination community were to take seriously Popper's views on theory testing, they might consider evidence that would challenge their belief in the harmfulness of vaccines. They might wonder whether rates of autism are higher among vaccinated than unvaccinated children. The fact that studies show that they are not is precisely the sort of "negative instance" that a confirmation bias prevents the antivaccination campaigners from taking seriously.

The conspiracy involving the connection between COVID-19 and 5G networks follows this exact same trajectory.[13] This time it was a doctor in Belgium who claimed, without any evidence, that the outbreak of the virus in Wuhan, China, was related to the recent construction of 5G towers. Although the newspaper that posted the doctor's report removed it only hours after determining it to be baseless, it was, as in the case of Wakefield's fraudulent study of vaccines, already too late. Conspiracy theorists once more saw a juicy bit of evidence confirming their distrust of the government, or large corporations, or new technology. Movie stars like Woody Harrelson and John Cusack fed the news to their fans, who, like the stars themselves, gave weight only to evidence that confirmed their attitude of general distrust rather than to evidence that might show 5G networks to be harmless. And once more, Russians filled the Internet with disinformation, filling the heads of conspiracy theorists with just the words that would confirm their belief in a connection between COVID-19 and 5G networks. And if the government insists that the 5G network is safe? This too confirms the belief that it is not, because for a conspiracy theorist this is exactly what a malevolent government would say. Negative instances—cases in which COVID-19 runs rampant in a community that is nowhere near a 5G tower, or cases in which a community around a 5G tower shows no signs of viral infection, or assurances by knowledgeable authorities that 5G transmissions are unrelated to COVID-19—are ignored, discounted, or twisted in ways that would impress even the most creative astrologer.

Confirmation bias, as research shows, appears to be a prominent and persistent feature of human psychology.[14] People are strongly inclined toward evidence that confirms their beliefs rather than to evidence that might refute them. But even if this tendency is in some sense a "hardwired" aspect of our psychology, the bad thinking it engenders is by no means unavoidable. Natural selection has endowed us with other proclivities, such as a sweet tooth, that we can resist. Deciding against a second slice of cake requires, for many, an act of willpower. Saying no might be difficult, but it is far from impossible. Willpower can be as effective in combating confirmation bias. It requires only that you keep in mind Bacon's admonishment that you be "indifferent" to positive and negative evidence. Instead of constantly asking, "What else supports my belief?," ask also "What evidence tells against my belief?" Certainly you need positive evidence to justify your belief, but you also need an absence of negative evidence.

The Base Rate Fallacy

So far we have been examining only one of the ingredients involved in abductive reasoning. When Holmes justifies his belief that Watson had spent time in Afghanistan, his thinking involves two elements: the observations he made regarding Watson's appearance, and the hypothesis he drew on the basis of these observations. Concerns about confirmation bias focus on the first element. Confirmation bias leads to bad thinking because it discourages people from giving serious consideration to observations that challenge their conclusions. But careful attention must be paid not only to the kinds of observations that participate in an inference to the best explanation but also to the characteristics of the hypothesis supported by these observations. Hypotheses, the "explanation part" of an inference to the best explanation, are not all created equal. Understanding why some hypotheses need more support than others is crucial to avoid bad thinking.

Suppose you spend some time chatting with a stranger at a bar. After a while you have made the following observations: the person leans toward the conservative end of the political spectrum, professes a healthy respect for authority, owns a gun, works out regularly, and is divorced. Putting on your Sherlock Holmes hat and reasoning abductively, which of these two explanations strike you as the better inference: (1) the person is a police officer, or (2) the person is a schoolteacher? If you think that inference to the best explanation favors the first option, you are guilty of bad thinking.

Before explaining why inference to the best explanation in fact justifies the second hypothesis—that the person is a schoolteacher—it is helpful look at a classic example from the literature on probabilistic reasoning. The example might seem unrelated to the question about the person in the bar, but it is not. The experimenters presented subjects with the following problem:

> A cab was involved in a hit and run accident at night. Two cab companies, the Green and the Blue, operate in the city. 85% of the cabs in the city are Green and 15% are Blue.
>
> A witness identified the cab as Blue. The court tested the reliability of the witness under the same circumstances that existed on the night of the accident and concluded that the witness correctly identified each one of the two colors 80% of the time and failed 20% of the time.
>
> What is the probability that the cab involved in the accident was Blue rather than Green knowing that this witness identified it as Blue?[15]

As stated, this problem is very difficult for most people to solve. In fact, investigators have not only suggested that susceptibility to the confirmation bias is an evolved trait, but they have also speculated that evolution has made it hard for us to think about probabilities.[16] Many people presented with this problem judge the probability that a blue cab was involved in the accident to be 80 percent, apparently ignoring the information about the percentage of blue cabs in the city and focusing only on the reliability of the witness. The mistake these people make is not to attend to the proportion, or base rate, of blue cabs in the city. They commit the "base rate fallacy."

Another way to think about this question makes the correct answer easier to understand. Instead of putting the various figures in terms of percentages, imagine instead that a city has one hundred cabs, eighty-five of which are green and fifteen are blue. If you knew nothing about the reliability of the witness who reports the accident and were told only that an accident had occurred, you would be correct in thinking that a green cab was much more likely to have been involved in the accident than a blue cab. With eighty-five green cabs zipping around the city and only fifteen blue cabs, chances are much greater that a green cab will have hit a pedestrian than that a blue cab has. In fact, all else being equal, the chance that any given accident is caused by a green cab is 85 percent, because that is the proportion of green cabs in the city. If this still seems opaque, then change the numbers. Suppose that of the one hundred cabs in the city, ninety-nine are green and only one is blue. Now when you hear about a hit-and-run accident involving a cab, you should be very confident that a green cab was at fault. The base rate of green cabs—the proportion of green cabs in the city—is so much higher than the base rate of blue cabs that almost certainly it was a green cab that ran into someone.

The next piece of information concerns the reliability of the witness. Again, we can remove the percentage describing the witness's reliability in order to make the claim easier to understand. To say that the witness is 80 percent reliable means that if the witness were to see one hundred green cabs, she would correctly identify eighty of them as green and would mis-identify twenty of them as blue. Likewise, if she were to see one hundred blue cabs, she would correctly identify eighty of them as blue but would misidentify twenty of them as green. Now, returning to the example, if she were to see eighty-five green cabs, she would correctly identify sixty-eight of them as green $(85 \times 0.8 = 68)$, thereby misidentifying the remaining seventeen as blue. Moreover, if she were to see fifteen blue cabs, she would correctly identify twelve of them as blue $(15 \times 0.8 = 12)$ and would misidentify the other three as green. If you now count up all the cabs that the witness in the example *says* are blue, you get the twelve that she has correctly identified but also the sev-enteen green cabs that she has been misidentified as blue. In total, then, of the one hundred cabs in the city, the witness would say twenty-nine of them are blue. But, because only twelve of the cabs that the witness would identify as blue actu-ally are blue, the witness makes a correct identification only twelve twenty-ninths of the time. That means that the chance that the witness is correct is only 41 percent.

The lesson is that people often fail to think about base rates even in cases when the base rate makes an important difference to what you should believe. Should you believe the witness who says that the cab involved in the hit-and-run accident was blue? If all you knew about the witness was that she is reliable 80 percent of the time, you lack the information you need to decide whether to believe her report. Facts about the reliability of the witness are worthless unless combined with information about the proportion of blue and green cabs in the city. This point generalizes in surprising ways. For instance, a test for a disease that is 99 percent reliable might still be very misleading if the base rate of the disease in the population—the number of people who actually have the disease—is very small. If a disease affects only one in every one hundred thousand people, then a test that correctly identifies 99 percent of those people who have the disease, but says falsely that 1 percent of healthy people also have the disease, would be right only about one in one thousand times. This is because 99,999 people out of 100,000 do not have the disease, and the 1 percent of these people whom the test misidentifies as sick amounts to almost one thousand people. So, for every sick person the test correctly identifies as having the disease, it misidentifies about one thousand healthy people as also having it.

When you infer that the person at the bar with whom you have been speaking is a police officer, you have let stereotypes guide your thinking. The observations you have made seem to fit the image of a police officer better than they do a teacher. This is why the inference appears reasonable on its surface. Psychologists would say that you are reasoning "heuristically." You are relying on "quick and dirty" rules of thumb to justify a conclusion. The person at the bar displays many of the qualities that seem representative of police officers, so you jump to the conclusion that this is the person's profession. If the person had expressed an interest in literature or history, worn glasses, and complained (justifiably!) about being overworked and underpaid then you might have inferred that the person was a teacher.

But abductive inferences like these are not immune to facts about base rates.[17] Even though the person has characteristics that appear to be more representative of police officers than teachers, until you know the base rate of police officers and teachers in the population, you should be very cautious about drawing conclusions on the basis of how the person appears. One way to think about this is to regard facts about base rates as among the observations that your inference to the best explanation must include. You have observed that the person is politically conservative, owns a gun, and so forth. But you should also count among your observations the fact that in the United States there are about 3.2 million teachers and seven hundred thousand police officers. Until you include the fact that teachers outnumber police officers roughly 4.5 to 1, you cannot draw the most justified conclusion about the person's profession. Given this ratio, an inference to the best explanation now favors the belief that the person is a teacher.

The taxicab example yields another moral. We have seen that the reliability of a witness is only one factor that you must tally when deciding how much confidence to place in the witness's testimony. Given that only 15 percent of the cabs are blue, a witness who correctly identifies the color of a cab 80 percent of the time should be trusted only 41 percent of the time when claiming to have seen a blue cab. We can re-describe this idea in a way that makes clearer its relevance to Holmes's inference to the best explanation about Watson's recent whereabouts. Think of the witness's report as evidence in support of a hypothesis—a conclusion—about the color of a cab. When the witness says that the cab was blue, this observation provides support for the belief that it is blue. But, given the small proportion of blue cabs in the city, the imperfect reliability of the witness makes the hypothesis about the color of the cab only 41 percent likely. The fact that only 15 percent of cabs are blue is like an anchor that drags down the value of the witness's testimony. The less likely the hypothesis, the farther the value of the testimony sinks. On the other hand, the more likely the hypothesis, the less it detracts from the value of the testimony. If, for instance, the witness had said that the color of the cab was green rather than blue, the testimony would be far more compelling. The witness's reliability remains 80 percent, but the initial likelihood of the hypothesis is much higher, because 85 percent of the cabs in the city are green. Using the same reasoning that shows the witness would successfully identify blue cabs only 41 percent of the time, we can calculate that the witness's rate of success for identifying green cabs is close to 96 percent.

So, the justification that evidence provides for a conclusion is hostage to how likely the conclusion is even prior to looking for evidence in its support. A hypothesis with a very low initial chance of being correct will diminish the value of the evidence in its favor. This is why, although the person at the bar seems more like a police officer than a teacher, the safer inference is that the person is a teacher. The much smaller chance that any given person is a police officer than a teacher drags down the evidential value of the observations you have made about the person's character.

Fortunately, this relationship between the plausibility of a hypothesis and the evidential worth of the observations in its favor suggests a strategy when faced with a hypothesis with a low probability. We have seen that a witness with a steady reliability of 80 percent is much more likely to be correct when reporting on a highly likely event (that the accident involved a green cab) than on an unlikely event (that the accident involved a blue cab). But if we want to assure ourselves that the accident was indeed caused by a blue cab, the thing to do is to find more or better witnesses. Suppose the court interviewed a witness who is correct about a cab's color 95 percent of the time rather than 80 percent. The fact that only 15 percent of the cabs are blue will still drag down the value of this testimony, but because the testimony is more reliable to begin with, it will not sink as far. A witness who is 95 percent reliable, when reporting that the cab was blue, will be correct about 75 percent of the time. In a similar way you can compensate for the lower probability of encountering a police officer than a teacher. The analogue to a better witness in this case is the acquisition of more diagnostic observations. For instance, if you notice a badge on the person's lapel, or an officer's hat hanging from the back of the person's chair, your confidence that the person is a police officer should swell.

How does this discussion bear on Holmes's inference regarding Watson? Holmes seems to be relying on stereotypes or assumptions about representativeness no less than you did if you inferred that the person in the bar is a police officer. Whether the observations Holmes makes about Watson's appearance actually provide good support for his belief about Watson's origins depends on a number of factors—for instance, the proportion of medical doctors in Britain and the proportion of British citizens who served in Afghanistan. If very few British citizens are doctors who have served in Afghanistan, then the evidential value of Holmes's observations drops precipitously. Had Holmes included facts about base rates within his observations, he might not have expressed his conclusions with such supreme confidence.

To return to our main theme: conspiracy theorists are often as oblivious to the lessons to be drawn from the base rate fallacy as they are to those emerging from studies of the confirmation bias. One of the most outspoken promulgators of the idea that the Sandy Hook school shooting was staged happens to be a productive professional philosopher. And yet, despite his academic credentials, with a résumé that includes a number of important contributions to the philosophy of science, he appears unable to appreciate how the very low probability of the hypothesis he favors about Sandy Hook makes his evidence basically worthless. Thinking he might convince an interviewer that the unspeakably tragic events at Sandy Hook were a ruse, he asked: "What is the probability that six Ph.D.s would look at the evidence around Sandy Hook and all conclude it is a hoax?" The interviewer's response was just right: "I ask him what the probability is that every level of government and law enforcement and media is in on a hoax and that hundreds of people who knew the 26 victims and all the survivors have been lying for years."[18]

This same kind of response works just as effectively against people who assert that the entire COVID-19 epidemic is a government-driven hoax. Writing in his weekly ethics column for the *New York Times Magazine*, the philosopher Kwame Anthony Appiah highlights the absurdity of this idea to someone whose friend has endorsed the COVID-19 conspiracy theory:

> Your friend believes in an astonishingly complex conspiracy. It would involve a secret deal between Donald Trump and Xi Jinping and dozens of other political leaders on every habitable continent—people who haven't managed to coordinate their plans on lots of other important matters, like climate change. It would involve doctors in Geneva at the World Health Organization, in Atlanta at the C.D.C. and in hospitals all around the world conspiring with data scientists at Johns Hopkins to produce a fantastic flow of fake information. Or, if your friend thinks that everything those politicians and scientists and health workers appear to be saying is itself made up, it would require an even more amazing capacity on someone's part to control the media and the internet. And what possible purpose could it serve? You might as well propose that we are all living in the Matrix—though if we are, it isn't just the pandemic that's imaginary.[19]

In our discussion of the base rate fallacy, we saw that the initially low probability that a blue cab was involved in an accident should make you doubt any less-than-perfect witness who claims to have seen a blue cab hit a pedestrian. The alternative explanation of the accident, that it was caused by a green cab, is far more likely. We should be much more confident in the same witness's report had she testified to seeing a green cab rather than a blue cab. But the "theory" that the Sandy Hook massacre did not really happen and the claim the COVID-19 pandemic is a hoax are *incredibly* unlikely, for just the reasons that the reporter and Appiah make explicit. Almost certainly some other theory is true, just as it was almost certainly a green cab rather than a blue cab that hit the pedestrian. Presumably, the more likely explanation of the Sandy Hook shooting was that Adam Lanza did in fact murder the children and staff members; and the more likely explanation of the extensive reporting of thousands killed by COVID-19 is that thousands *were* killed by COVID-19. Anyone who wishes to justify the conspiracy theories about Sandy Hook and COVID-19 faces a nearly insurmountable task. In order to overcome the reality that their theories are staggeringly improbable, they must present a bounty of evidence far greater than would be required for the more likely theories—that Lanza was to blame, and that COVID-19 is real.

Understood in this light, the lesson from our discussion of the base rate fallacy reflects little more than common sense. If your first-grader returns from school one day reporting that there had been a fire drill, we do not question the claim, even though first-graders may not be the most reliable witnesses. On the other hand, if the child reports that extraterrestrials had invaded the school, we should wonder. The child's reliability may be the same on each occasion. Why, then, ask for more evidence before believing the second report? Simply because alien invasions are far less likely than fire drills. It is bad thinking to treat all theories—all explanations of the data—as on a par with respect to the amount of evidence required to justify our beliefs in them. Conspiracy theories score so low in their initial credibility that evidence must work much harder to support them over their more likely alternatives.

Toward Better Reasoning

Philosophers divide all reasoning into one of two categories. It is either deductive or nondeductive. When you aim to justify a belief with deductive reasoning, you must be careful to construct a valid argument. If you are sure that your argument has a valid form, and if you can establish the truth of the premises in the argument, then you can be certain that your conclusion is true. There is no higher standard of justification than what a sound deductive argument provides. More typically, though, justification will rely on nondeductive reasoning. Nondeductive reasoning does not guarantee the absolute certainty that sound deductive reasoning does, but it remains a powerful source of justification nonetheless.

There are many varieties of nondeductive reasoning, but we have examined two of the most common. Enumerative inductive reasoning draws conclusions on the basis of observations made on a sample of instances. There is a danger facing this sort of reasoning when the samples on which conclusions are based are too small. Patterns that appear in small samples may be the consequence of chance, like a sequence of heads in a series of only three coin flips. When you see a pattern in a small sample and offer a causal story to explain it, you are exercising bad thinking. The pattern is probably not real, and so the story you offer is probably false.

Another sort of nondeductive reasoning involves an inference from observations to an explanation for these observations.

Inference to the best explanation, or abduction, can be abused in various ways that produce distinctive kinds of bad thinking. When trying to defend a conclusion on the grounds that it is the best explanation for a collection of observations, it is important that you do not cherry-pick the observations, allowing into the collection only those that confirm the conclusion you desire. In order to avoid this confirmation bias, you need to think about evidence that would *disconfirm* your conclusion. When inferring to the *best* explanation, testing your beliefs against negative evidence is often the only way to know whether your explanation is indeed the best.

Proper application of abductive reasoning also requires you to think about the probability, or reasonableness, of the belief you wish to defend. If the belief is unlikely to begin with, this raises the bar on the amount or quality of evidence that is necessary to justify it. A far-fetched belief will require a lot more evidence for its justification than a less remarkable belief. You think badly when you do not permit information about base rates to inform your decisions about what to believe.

Chapter 4

When Bad Thinking Becomes Bad Behavior

The ancient Greek poet Archilochus, in a parable popularized by the philosopher and intellectual historian Isaiah Berlin, said "the fox knows many things, but the hedgehog knows one big thing."[1] Before the academic professionalization of philosophy in the nineteenth century, philosophers tended to be foxes. Rather than specializing in one area or another—metaphysics, epistemology, ethics—thinkers such as Plato, Aristotle, Aquinas, Descartes, Spinoza, Leibniz, Hume, and Kant, among so many others, took on all the big questions.

Among those quintessential philosophical topics—What is reality? What is knowledge? What is a good life?—there is the one about human nature itself: What is it to be a human being? Plato, ignorant of kangaroos, suggested that we are essentially featherless bipedal animals.[2] Aristotle, on the other hand, located our essence in the capacity to reason. He said that to be human is to be a *rational* animal, although he also famously claimed that "man is by nature a political animal," moved instinctively to organize with others into society.[3]

Putting this metaphysical debate about "essence" aside, we can say with certainty that human beings are *moral* animals— or, to put it better, "moral agents." We are, by our nature—and barring any relevant disabilities—endowed with the capacity of deliberation over action in the light of principles and values. When we choose to do something *because*, after thoughtful reflection, we believe it to be the right thing to do (or avoid it because we believe it to be the wrong thing to do), we are behaving as moral agents. But we are also exercising that fundamental human capacity when we choose to do something *despite* our seeing that it is the wrong thing to do, and even when we do it *because* we see that it is the wrong thing to do. As long as our action is deliberately chosen and informed, for better or for worse, by beliefs about principles and values that we understand and acknowledge—regardless of what those principles and values happen to be—we are acting as moral agents. The Nazi is no less a moral agent than the Good Samaritan.

Unfortunately, there are many ways for this process of thoughtful, informed practical reasoning to break down or go awry. As the Nazi example shows, exercising our moral agency to the fullest does not imply that we act well or do the right thing, or even that we *intend* to act well or do the right thing. But, more to the point, neither do we always exercise our moral capacities to the fullest. Even with the best of intentions, we can end up doing what, were we thinking properly and thinking well, we would not—and perhaps should not—do. We now know that good people, because of bad thinking, can be epistemically at fault; they often believe things without adequate justification. But good people, because of a different sort of bad thinking, can also *do* bad things. Perhaps more often, good people, because of bad thinking, simply fail to do a good thing.

Failures in Judgment

Consider the following examples:

In a Madison, Wisconsin, high school, a Black security guard is dealing with a disruptive student, who is also Black. While being led away by the guard, the student is repeatedly calling him a notorious racial slur. The guard tells the student several times "Do not call me a [N-word]," using the actual word. The school district, however, has a "zero-tolerance, one strike and you're out" policy governing the use of that word. It is a well-intentioned policy, instituted to ensure a safe and respectful learning environment for a diverse body of students. Unfortunately, it is also a policy that the security guard appears, purely as a technicality, to have violated, and he is summarily fired by the principal. (After a public outcry, the guard is later reinstated.)[4]

At a cross-country meet in Ohio, a sixteen-year-old Muslim woman is disqualified for wearing a hijab during the race. (She attends a private Muslim school but participates in athletics for the local public high school.) Because her coach neglected to fill out *before* the race the proper paperwork for a religious clothing waiver (which she would have received as a matter of course), she is told by the race directors—*after* the race—that her headwear (which, though made by Nike, brings her no competitive advantage) violates regulations governing athletic uniforms. She had run her personal best time in the race.[5]

In a New York City grocery store, an elderly man with a walker approaches the checkout counter with a bottle of wine and other items. The man is clearly well above the drinking age of twenty-one. But because he does not have a photo ID proving his assertion that he is at least five decades older than the state's legal minimum for the sale of alcoholic beverages, he is told he may not purchase the wine. If he wants the wine, he must go home, retrieve his driver's license or some other form of identification, and return to the store.[6]

Something has gone seriously wrong in all three of these cases—and there must be many such episodes occurring every day, in every part of the world. It is related to the epistemic stubbornness we have already examined, but it goes beyond that. It is not just a matter of certain individuals persisting stubbornly either in inadequately justified beliefs or, worse, in beliefs that the evidence clearly falsifies. There is an ethical failure here, due not to malice or vice but to a failure of thinking well.

What we see in all three cases is an overzealous, even thoughtless application of a rule. In the first two cases, it leads to what any reasonable person should regard as wrongheaded and even unjust treatment; in the third case, the way the situation is handled is senseless and silly (and, for the elderly gentleman, highly inconvenient and troublesome). The problem is that the rule-enforcers are not thinking hard enough about what they are doing, and therefore they are acting unreasonably.

Laws, regulations, rules, and principles—whether civil, moral, commercial, athletic, or some other sort—are by their nature general. They have to be, to cover effectively a large number and broad range of circumstances and cases. As the philosopher and legal theorist H.L.A. Hart explains in his classic work *The Concept of Law*, no society could possibly work if its members had to be separately and directly informed by some representative of the sovereign authority whether their actions were permitted or forbidden. You cannot expect the holder of executive office to have to determine in every single case whether people may or may not do what they intend to do. The problem is not just one of timing or communication. Equally unworkable would be a generally and publicly accessible list of actions that specifies what each particular individual is allowed to do under what circumstances and when. Such a list would be, if not infinite, practically endless, as its drafters would have to foresee every possible kind of action under every conceivable circumstance. Instead of a body of highly specific edicts indexed to individuals and their situations, we rely on laws, what Hart calls "general forms of directions which do not name, and are not addressed to, particular individuals, and do not indicate a particular act to be done." Hence, the "standard form" of laws is general in two ways: "It indicates a general type of conduct and applies to a general class of persons who are expected to see that it applies to them and to comply with it. . . . The range of persons affected and the manner in which the range is indicated may vary with different legal systems and even different laws. In a modern state it is normally understood that, in the absence of special indications widening or narrowing the class, the general laws extend to all persons within its territorial boundaries."[7]

Laws, while general, will still be more or less particular. Some civil laws, for example, are directed at all citizens no matter what their circumstances—for example, laws concerning the most egregious forms of criminal behavior. The law against murder or theft applies to everyone. Other kinds of laws are directed only at individuals who satisfy certain conditions—for example, if they are authorized and active participants in some organized practice. The balk rule of baseball specifies that the pitcher on the mound with the ball in his hand may not fake a pitch or a throw (to fool a base runner) if his foot is on the rubber. This rule, while not naming any particular player or team, applies only to people who are actually engaged in playing the game, and only some of them (the pitchers); players who are not pitchers, and people who are not even playing baseball, can do whatever they want on the mound. Still, even if the domain of a law or rule is specifically restricted in this way, there must be some degree of generality; otherwise we are not talking about a practice-governing "law" proper. It cannot be that only a certain relief pitcher for the New York Yankees is not allowed to fake the throw. That would not really be a law at all but something more like an arbitrary stipulation.

Moreover, to preserve their generality and practicality, laws must be relatively simple and straightforward. Their purpose—not always successfully accomplished—is to prescribe or proscribe ways of acting in a clear and unambiguous manner. This purpose would be thwarted if laws were complicated by having conditions and exceptions explicitly built into them. The law does not say, "Do not drive over the speed limit, unless you are heading to the hospital for an emergency and are a really good driver." It says, "Do not drive over the speed limit, period."

While laws are general, the human beings to whom they apply are highly particular. It goes without saying that their conditions, needs, desires, preferences and circumstances vary in innumerable ways. Even so, human behavior does tend to fall neatly under laws in relevant respects. Rich or poor, good driver or bad, in a Porsche or an old Volkswagen Beetle, once you take control of a moving automobile you are a driver, and if you are speeding you have violated a traffic law. And no matter who you are, where you live, and what your material or spiritual needs might be, you may not engage in extortion, perjury, or insider trading.

The relative generality and simplicity of laws and rules means that their implementation and enforcement require mediation. Someone (or, in our automated age, something) has to determine the applicability of a law or rule to a particular case, as well as the propriety of actually applying it. This is, of course, the responsibility of police officers, security guards, judges, regulators, inspectors, and others who are formally charged with overseeing compliance either with public laws or the rules and regulations at work in private sectors (managers in factories, umpires and referees in sport leagues). But it is also something that everyone will have to do on many occasions throughout their lives, particularly (but not necessarily) if they have some special expertise or authority. Surgeons need to determine whether a medical procedure that is generally prescribed for a certain condition is appropriate in a given case; teachers have to enforce rules of decorum in their classrooms; owners of grocery stores must decide if there are occasions when there is no need to demand an ID; and parents cannot avoid situations in which they have to choose between enforcing a rule they have laid down and making an exception.

This is where the trouble begins.

The Relevance of Difference

As we have seen, the particularities and peculiarities, major or minor, that make for the rich variety of human behavior are typically irrelevant when it is time to decide whether to enforce a law. If you are speeding, your height, weight, income, and musical talents do not matter. If you are underage, then the fashionable clothes you are wearing when you try to buy liquor will be of no exculpatory help.

Still, differences *do* sometimes make a difference. There will be occasions when they *are* relevant, when taking account of the particularities of an individual and her situation is quite appropriate, even obligatory for those charged with implementing the law—if not from a legal perspective then from a moral or practical one. This is where judgment, as distinct from the sort of rational faculties that have been our concern so far, comes in.

Even in the simplest and most straightforward cases, the administration of a law or the application of a rule always requires judgment. Knowing the relevant law or rule is the easy part for those charged with its enforcement. This is something that it is assumed they bring to every situation. A police officer is expected to be familiar with the statutes that govern her bailiwick. A security guard should know the regulations of the shopping mall where he works—for example, what type of behavior counts as shoplifting and what to do if someone is seen engaging in it. Sports umpires must have the rules of their respective sports ready in mind in order to make quick and often difficult judgments in the heat of competition.

A slightly more challenging part of any enforcement job is having the relevant empirical information at hand. You need to determine the particular circumstances in which you are now called upon to apply the law or regulation. You must establish precisely what happened and then assess whether the event actually falls under the rule. Was the car being driven by the person suspected of driving it, was he driving it in a zone with a maximum speed limit, and was the car indeed going over the limit? What clothing and gear was the athlete wearing, was that gear prohibited by the rules of the event, and did she fail to seek a waiver before the event? Did the shopper slip the shoes into her bag and try to walk out of the store without paying for them? Did the football player's foot touch out of bounds after he made the catch? Determining any of this can be a relatively easy task, when the law is clear and the relevant circumstances or behavior evident and undisputed. "Yes, officer, as your radar gun indicates, I was driving my car over the posted speed limit." Any ambiguities or doubts on the empirical question can be resolved by closer inspection—for example, photographic evidence or video review. While there is an element of judgment involved, it remains primarily a matter of ascertaining the facts.

The most difficult question involving judgment—and, for our purposes here, the important and morally fraught one—is whether in this instance the law or rule *should* be invoked and *how* it should be enforced. Assuming that the law or rule is known by both the enforcer and the perpetrator, and assuming that both parties agree on the basic facts of what happened—that the individual is technically in violation of the relevant law—a decision remains to be made concerning whether to enforce the law or rule in the circumstances. Quite often, there really is, and should be, no choice in the matter. A thief ought to be apprehended and prosecuted; a sport referee who chooses to look the other way at a flagrant foul will pay a heavy price for his leniency. However, there are also occasions when someone must decide if there is some value to overlooking a violation, and whether that value is greater than the value of enforcing the law.

Knowing What to Do and When to Do It

Judgment is a matter of discretion. A discreet person knows where and when not to say or do something. She is good at assessing an individual or situation and determining what is called for in word and deed. By contrast, an indiscreet person will typically say or do the wrong thing, something inappropriate or offensive.

Judgment in the moral sphere is a matter of reasonable discrimination. A person with good judgment recognizes both what is typical *and* what is distinctive about the particular case at hand, and then notes whether what is distinctive is relevant. The fact that the man in the grocery store was obviously decades above the legal drinking age is relevant; the fact that the wine he wanted to buy was a Merlot is not. The teenage runner was indeed wearing a hijab for which her coach forgot to seek a waiver; what mattered was not the headscarf's brand or color, but whether it gave her a competitive advantage. Circumstances are everything. The police officer who declines to give a speeding ticket to a driver on his way to the hospital because his wife is in labor in the back seat is making a judgment call.

Philosophers have long insisted on the complexity of our moral lives.[8] Determining, in quiet moments of armchair reflection, what is in principle right or wrong is difficult enough; knowing what you ought to do in the press of immediate circumstances is even harder. There are often many factors to consider, and doing one thing that seems to be (and maybe is) right can require that you neglect some other duty. Providing urgent help to a stranger may force you to break a promise to meet a dear friend who requires counsel. Antigone, in Sophocles's tragedy, must choose between her personal and religious duty to bury her dead brother and her civic obligation to obey the leader Creon's command that the traitor's body should be left to the vultures. Her moral conflict is real.[9] Circumstances may be such that we cannot possibly satisfy all of our duties, much less all our desires. Sometimes the best we can do is opt for the lesser of two evils.

Traditionally, philosophers, troubled by such apparent complexity, aspired to reduce ethics to a single, ultimate principle, the quasi-mechanical application of a rule that is supposed to provide a unique, unambiguous, and morally correct answer in every situation. For utilitarians like the British moral philosophers Jeremy Bentham (1748–1832) and John Stuart Mill (1806–73), it is the principle of utility, or maximizing happiness: you should always do the action whose anticipated outcome is a net increase in the well-being of all who are affected by the action. Immanuel Kant (1724–1804), on the other hand, for whom consequences are morally irrelevant when determining the rightness or wrongness of an action, insisted that the operative principle is an absolutely unconditional moral command, or "categorical imperative": you should always act in such a way that you, as a purely rational moral agent, regardless of your personal inclinations or preferences, could imagine that acting in this way should be an absolute law holding for everybody. Simply put: what if everyone did that? Can you reasonably envision that all people should be directed (or even allowed) to do what you are going to do? If you cannot, then the action is morally wrong and you ought not to do it. Kant gives the example of making false promises. No reasonable person could envision a universal law that allows making a false promise or telling a lie when it is convenient and in one's own interest to do so.

However, such simplicity and uniqueness of principle is neither desirable nor practical. This strategy for finding absolute rules can easily lead to results that are, intuitively, morally problematic, even objectionable. The Kantian principle, for example, generates the absolute moral duty never to make a false promise or tell a lie, since no rational agent could possibly envision a universal law that allows all people to make false promises or tell lies when it is convenient for them to do so. Such a law would be self-defeating, and thus irrational; it would render false promises and lies themselves impossible, since the trust required for these sorts of deceptions would be undermined. In a world in which false promises and lies are morally permitted, even encouraged, no one would ever believe what anyone else says. However, Kant's absolute principle, notoriously, is supposed to apply even to situations where the outcome of telling the truth is morally abhorrent—for example, when Nazis come to your door in Amsterdam in 1943 demanding to know whether you are hiding a Jewish family in your home.

No single rule can possibly accommodate the variety and complexity of situations in which human agents are required to act and the expectations they are called upon to meet; and when there are multiple rules in play, they may clash. Sometimes there are clear limits to utilitarian reasoning, strong moral reasons not to engage in an action no matter how much happiness that action would generate.[10] The enslavement of a minority population is, in principle, morally impermissible, regardless of how happy it would make the majority. A medical doctor should never harvest the organs of an unwitting healthy patient even if she might save five lives through transplant surgeries. On the other hand, sometimes there are good utilitarian reasons to violate what had seemed an absolute moral proscription. A lie that saves a life or even simply eases a friend's suffering may be permissible. You ought to break your promise to meet a friend for coffee if your sick parent needs to be taken to the hospital. Sometimes there is no available rule whatsoever, and we have to rely on deep-seated moral intuitions, or even just feelings of love or kindness, for guidance on what to do. Moral agency cannot consist simply in the rote application of a universal principle.

This is where judgment comes in. It goes beyond knowing which rule, if any, might pertain to the situation. Deciding the right thing to do, which can include a willingness to bend the relevant rule or even a refusal to invoke it altogether, is a matter of using one's own sense of justice and fairness. Judgment demands consideration and the exercise of discretion.

Exercising judgment differs from either ignoring the rule or overlooking the facts and, in effect, turning the other way. When we turn the other way, we are essentially refusing to make a judgment one way or the other and thereby abdicating responsibility. By contrast, judgment involves acknowledging that the rule has been broken, that the perpetrating party is technically guilty, but also making a conscious and deliberate choice not to enforce the rule. Just as important, and unlike turning the other way, you must be prepared, if challenged, to defend that choice with reasons. It is to recognize that the full application of the rule would result in an unjust, or at least undesirable, state of affairs.

The Madison school authorities, the Ohio race referees, and the owner of that grocery store could have, and should have, exercised judgment.[11] All three of these cases reflect a kind of stubbornness. It is not unrelated to the epistemic stubbornness that, as we have seen, consists in refusing to revise or even abandon a belief in the face of evidence that the belief is unjustified or false—something that amounts to irrationality, even a kind of stupidity. In the case of the school district, the cross-country meet, and the grocery store, however, the stubbornness being exhibited is not so much epistemic as it is practical and normative. Where the epistemically stubborn person holds on to a belief regardless of the compelling reasons against it, or refuses to adopt a belief regardless of the wealth of evidence in its favor, the *normatively* stubborn person enforces a rule no matter how obviously wrong and counterproductive doing so is in the present circumstances. He is inflexible, apparently indifferent to the original purpose of the rule as well as of the consequences of his obstinacy.

In our three examples, the inflexible rule followers are, like the epistemically stubborn person, guilty of a kind of bad thinking. They fail to reasonably assess their actions and reflect on why they are taking them. By the same token, they do not consider which actions they *should* take and why they *should* take them. They are not taking the opportunity to critically evaluate their behavior in the light of principles and values, whether their own moral principles or, perhaps more important, the principles and values of the institutions they are serving and that motivate the rule they are enforcing. In short, by not exercising judgment, they are acting blindly. The epistemically stubborn agent ignores canons of good reasoning; the normatively stubborn actor neglects principles of sound practical judgment.

Not all forms of normative stubbornness involve bad thinking. Obviously there are often good reasons to stand by and enforce a rule, even when doing so is difficult or entails some loss. Those of us who are parents can easily recall situations where enforcing a rule is more costly or frustrating or counterproductive than making an easy exception, but nonetheless justified, perhaps for the sake of setting a precedent or modeling good behavior. "No, you may not have a piece of cake just before dinner, no matter how much of a fuss you make." However, in the three cases we are considering, the normative stubbornness of the rule enforcers prevents them from seeing the well-meaning intentions that motivated the rule in the first place, and so consigns them to act not in accordance with the spirit of the rule, but only its letter. Nor do they recognize when an exception to the rule is not only perfectly harmless but even leads to some good or the prevention of something bad.

Aristotle recognized that discretion is an essential part of virtue. He argues in his ethical writings that the virtuous person—the person endowed with *areté*, the proper human excellence of reasoning in connection with thought and action—is good at intuitively sizing up her situation (as well as the situations of others) and choosing the proper action. That proper action, in Aristotle's account, is generally a mean between two extremes.[12] The charitable person, for example, avoids both stinginess and profligacy; she gives away neither too little nor too much. The brave person is neither cowardly nor foolhardy; she knows when to stand her ground and when to avoid a conflict. Moreover, what counts as "the mean" is usually relative to the person and her circumstances. The charitable mean for a Bill Gates or the queen of England would certainly be too much for a person of moderate wealth and impossible for someone living in poverty. A courageous move for a strong, young, well-trained individual would probably be reckless for a weak, elderly, or infirm person. It would be right, even morally obligatory, all things considered, for an expert swimmer to jump into a lake to save a drowning person; it would certainly not be obligatory—in fact, it would be stupid—for someone who cannot swim to do so. The virtuous person, demonstrating excellence in the exercise of practical reason, knows and does what is right and appropriate in the situation. She is good at exercising judgment.

Certainly life would be a lot more difficult if we were supposed to exercise judgment on every occasion in which we are called upon to act. After all, the point of rules is to simplify things so as to make them more tractable. Assessing the relevance of circumstances and likely consequences in applying a rule is not always possible, especially if the situation is complex and requires immediate action.[13] On the other hand, we give up a good deal of our responsibility as moral agents as soon as we surrender all our decision making to rules.[14]

On Weakness

There are many possible explanations for why people fail, or even deliberately refuse, to exercise judgment and do what they think—what they, in some sense, know—is right. Prejudice, laziness, and urgency may stand in the way of the rational reflection that judgment requires. Emotions too can prevent us from making exceptions to rules in order to do what is right, and sometimes this is perfectly understandable, even excusable. If it is a cashier in the grocery who demands an ID from the elderly man, then, despite any feelings of sympathy he may have for the gentleman and perhaps recognizing that enforcing the store's policy on this occasion is absurd, he may not have the authority to make an exception and allow him to buy his wine without an ID; in this case, the legitimate fear of losing his job compels him to follow the regulation, despite the ridiculousness of doing so.[15] (A manager or store owner who refuses to make the exception is in a very different situation.) It sometimes takes great fortitude and strength of mind, even courage, to exercise reasonable judgment in the face of passions such as fear, love, hate, and anger. All too often the passions win out.

One of the many tales in the ancient Roman poet Ovid's *Metamorphoses* concerns the tragic story of Jason and Medea. As the young woman hears the harsh terms that her father, King Aeëtes, sets for the Argonauts to claim the Golden Fleece, she fears the danger they pose for the man with whom she has fallen in love. Medea is torn between her feelings for Jason, whom she desperately wants to help, and loyalty to her father. With "reason powerless to master her passion," she eventually opts for love over duty.

> I am dragged along by a strange new force. Desire and
>   reason
> are pulling in different directions. I see the right way and
>   approve it,
> but follow the wrong.[16]

She does what she knows is wrong, but she cannot help herself.

Medea's internal struggle has been seen by philosophers as emblematic of a moral quandary that the ancient Greeks called *akrasia*—literally, "lack of power"—and that is often translated as "weakness (of will)" or "incontinence." *Akrasia* is the condition of an agent who knowingly and voluntarily acts contrary to her better judgment. In this clash between the nobler and worse angels of our nature, a person knows exactly what she ought to do and is even motivated to do it, and yet she somehow fails to follow through on that knowledge and desire and ends up acting otherwise.

In Medea's case, at least as Ovid depicts it, *akrasia* is a matter of reason being overpowered by passion. The mind says do one thing, but the heart ends up taking the person down a different path. This is, in fact, how many philosophers have explained the phenomenon. Plato, for example, divided the human soul into distinct parts, with weakness or incontinence explained by the baser part, appetite, leading the soul against the commands of the superior part, reason. In his dialogue *Phaedrus*, Plato's protagonist, Socrates, presents an allegory in which the soul is represented by a chariot drawn by two horses. The white horse is reason, seeking to take the chariot upward; the unruly black horse is appetite, pulling in the opposite direction. The driver of the chariot must struggle against the black horse—the urges of appetite—that drags the vehicle downward. The battle, Socrates explains in the dialogue, is between "an innate desire for pleasure" and "an acquired judgment that aims at what is best." Sometimes, he notes, "these internal guides are in accord, sometimes at variance; now one gains the mastery, now the other. And when judgment guides us rationally toward what is best, and has the mastery, that mastery is called temperance, but when desire drags us irrationally toward pleasure and has come to rule within us, the name given to that rule is wantonness."[17] Plato believed that *akrasia* was a real phenomenon, that sometimes people who know and are moved to do what is right nonetheless willingly act contrary to that knowledge.

The seventeenth-century philosopher Baruch (or Benedictus) Spinoza (1632–77) agreed with Plato, in a sense. Weakness or incontinence occurs when passion subverts rational choice by overpowering it. However, for Spinoza it is not a matter of some irrational desire for pleasure overriding or preventing us from carrying out the objective, unemotional commands of our rational nature. It is not body versus mind or undisciplined appetite versus cool, calm intellect. There is emotional power on both sides. Just like the pleasures, pains, and other sensations that we receive or anticipate from external things, the true ideas of reason have their own emotional force. Even rational ideas have a "feel" or endeavor that moves us. When an individual suffers from *akrasia*, a properly formed rational judgment about what is best is affectively too weak to overcome the emotional pull of a passionate desire for some other course of action. You might very much want to do the right thing, but that desire can be overpowered by the idea of some anticipated base pleasure. We end up acting against our better judgment because the enticement of immediate gratification wins out over our knowledge that our long-term interest is better served by refraining from the indulgence in question. This explains, for example, why a student would go out partying with friends rather than study for upcoming exams that she strongly wants to do well on. As Spinoza puts it, "a desire that arises from a true knowledge of good and evil can be extinguished or restrained by many other desires which arise from affects by which we are tormented."[18]

Akrasia of the sort that Plato and Spinoza describe is not really a matter of bad thinking. It is not that the person fails to sufficiently consider his principles and his actions and thus, in the absence of such rational reflection, lacks a properly justified belief as to the right thing to do and a desire to do it. Rather, his rational desire to do what he justifiably takes to be right ends up being no match for the power of his irrational desires. Good thinking and the exercise of judgment is no guarantee that one *will* do the right thing.

Aristotle, however, offers a somewhat different account of weakness or incontinence. In his view, it is not so much a matter of acting against our fully developed better judgment but rather of a failure of judgment and reasoning. For Aristotle, the incontinent agent does *not* act against his better judgment, mainly because he cannot form the correct judgment in the first place. Thus, as we shall see, the phenomenon Aristotle describes as *akrasia* does indeed seem to frame moral weakness as a model of bad thinking.

Aristotle calls the kind of thinking that ordinarily informs our behavior as moral agents "practical reasoning." It literally *is* a form of reasoning insofar as, when an agent deliberates on how to act, his thinking starts with certain premises and moves to a conclusion about action. It is very much like the kind of deductive reasoning that we examined in chapter 3. Aristotle offers the following example: "I need a covering and a cloak is a covering, and so I need a cloak. What I need I ought to make, I need a cloak, and so I ought to make a cloak."[19] Aristotle does not think that every agent explicitly and consciously engages in such an interior logical argument whenever he acts. Rather, the syllogism is meant simply to capture, in a formal way, the more spontaneous mental processes of someone who deliberates and chooses a course of action.

When practical reasoning is done well, Aristotle calls the virtue at work *phronesis*, sometimes translated as "intelligence." Intelligence is not theoretical or scientific knowledge but a kind of intellectually informed pragmatic skill. "An intelligent person," he says, "is able to deliberate finely about what is good and beneficial for himself, not about some restricted area—e.g. about what promotes health or strength—but about what promotes living well in general. . . . Intelligence is a state grasping the truth, involving reason, concerned with action about what is good or bad for a human being."[20] *Phronesis* is essentially good judgment with respect to behavior. Its objective is right action aiming at a good end. The intelligent person perceives with perfect certainty the best action to take. She does this by validly drawing conclusions—not theoretical or speculative conclusions but practical ones, imperatives or commands to action—from true premises and then, if all goes well, acts on the basis of her knowledge of "what is good or bad."[21]

The reasoning of a person exercising *phronesis* begins with some general principle or claim. This serves as the "major" or universal premise. One such premise might be "healthy food is good for human beings." But the intelligent person is also especially skilled at sizing up particular cases, recognizing their salient features, and then subsuming them under the general principle. She will thus know that this vegetarian meal in front of her is an instance of healthy food; this particular claim serves as the "minor" premise in the syllogism. She will then deductively conclude that it is therefore good to eat the meal (and hence, all things being equal, she will eat it).

In general terms, practical reasoning in the intelligent person begins with a goal to be achieved—not just any goal, but a goal that she has correctly identified as good and worthwhile for a human being. She will then discover the most effective way to achieve that goal. "Virtue makes the goal correct, and intelligence makes what promotes the goal [correct]."[22] The person who is merely clever but lacks *phronesis* is also skilled at achieving the goals he sets for himself; however, his goals are not always good. "If the goal is fine," Aristotle says, "cleverness is praiseworthy; if the goal is base, cleverness is unscrupulousness."[23]

The intelligent person thus excels in deliberation and choice over different courses of action. She has an exceptional sense of judgment. She takes her conception of the good and sees exactly what it calls for in the immediate situation. In short, she knows the correct goal and how to achieve it. In this way she does the right thing. And she does what is right not accidentally, but deliberately and in an informed way. By contrast, things do not always work out so well for those who are less than virtuous and do not exercise *phronesis*. Sometimes, Aristotle notes, our practical reasoning goes awry, and we end up acting contrary to what is best.

Aristotle's account of *akrasia* is notoriously difficult and full of ambiguities.[24] The incontinent person is supposed to be someone who knows he is acting wrongly. But, then, why does he do it? And in what sense does he "know" his action is wrong? How is he acting contrary to his better judgment?

Sometimes Aristotle's explanation of weakness appears similar to that of Plato and Spinoza. It is not that we fail to reason properly and thus lack full knowledge of the right action but that this fine rational cognition is no match for strong appetites for bodily or other pleasures pulling us in a different direction. Aristotle initially defines incontinence as "when people go to excess, in conflict with the correct reason in them, in the pursuit of pleasure." This happens even when we know fully well right from wrong, but reason, though well deployed, is "overcome" by the desire for food, sex, and other enticements.[25]

At other times, however, desires may corrupt reason's proper operation. In this case, the failure to act well is indeed the result of an epistemic shortcoming—an inadequacy of knowledge and a failure to reason well, although an inadequacy and failure that is ultimately caused by the undue influence of passion or appetite. This is the condition of what Aristotle calls the "impetuous" individual: "One type of incontinence is impetuosity, while another is weakness. For the weak person deliberates, but then his feeling makes him abandon the result of his deliberation; but the impetuous person is led on by his feelings because he has not deliberated."[26] Aristotle is fond of saying that the incontinent person who is impetuous does have knowledge, but only "in a way." He has all the relevant items that are needed for effective practical reasoning: he understands the universal principle, and he apprehends the particularities of the present case. However, he is not fully able to activate and apply this knowledge. There are many things—being "asleep or mad or drunk" or "emotions, sexual appetite"—that can "disturb knowledge" and prevent a person from fully grasping some relevant fact, or make him incapable of either deliberating properly or putting that knowledge to work in the right way. "The incontinent person is not in the condition of someone who knows and is attending [to his knowledge, as he would have to be if he had intelligence], but in the condition as if asleep or drunk."[27]

Overcome by the cravings of gluttony or suffering the pangs of hunger, the impetuously incontinent person can go wrong in a number of ways: either he does not attend to his general knowledge of good and bad foods, or he fails to recognize the harmfulness of the food presently in front of him—a sugar-laden dessert—or he does not draw the conclusion that this present food is not something he should be eating. Similarly, someone in the throes of lustful passion may not be able to think properly and recognize what is best to do, and thus will fail to resist the lure of an adulterous liaison. The knowledge is there, so to speak, but misguided yearnings hinder or render it inactive. So yes, the person *in a sense* does know that his action is wrong, and thus is *sort of* acting against his better judgment, but in a sense he does not know: "The knowledge that is present when someone is affected by incontinence, and that is dragged about because he is affected [by appetite], is not the sort [of knowledge] that seems to be knowledge to the full extent. . . . So much, then, for knowing and not knowing, and for how it is possible to know and still act incontinently."[28] The incontinent person, so conceived, is acting contrary to his "better judgment" because he is doing something that is contrary to the judgment he *would* make if all his beliefs about good and bad and right and wrong and all his perceptions about particular things—including whatever he needs to know about the present circumstances—were active and playing their proper role in careful practical reasoning.

Aristotle's view may, in the end, be not unlike that of Socrates.[29] Plato's philosophical mentor reportedly disagreed with his student and argued that no one knowingly and willingly does what is wrong. If you fail to do what is good, it is because you are lacking some essential information—perhaps either a general principle about the kinds of things that are good or the fact that some particular item is in fact one of those good things. Here are the words that Plato puts in Socrates's mouth in one of his dialogues: "When people make a wrong choice of pleasures and pains—that is, of good and evil—the cause of their mistake is lack of knowledge. . . . What being mastered by pleasure really is, is ignorance."[30] For Socrates, knowing the good entails doing the good. Perhaps for Aristotle, too, if you have unhindered, active knowledge and you properly carry out the process of practical reasoning to its prescriptive conclusion, you will necessarily do the right thing. If you really do *know*, in the fullest sense of the term, the general principle that, with an exam the next day, it is better to study than watch TV; if you also have in mind all the relevant information about your particular situation (your lack of preparedness for the exam, the importance of getting a good grade on it, and so on); and if you put all of that together in the proper way and reason to the correct practical conclusion, then you will study, no matter what other desires you may happen to have.

"Why Should *I* Do It?"

The problem of *akrasia* or weakness—why would a person act contrary to his better judgment and fail to do what he knows to be right—should be distinguished from a related but nonetheless different problem: the problem of motivation. In the problem of motivation, the question is whether it is possible to know the right action and yet not be motivated to do it. With weakness, the assumption is that the person *is* motivated to do what is right—Medea feels the pull of duty to her father and a desire to submit to his authority—but this motivation gives way to an opposing impulse. By contrast, one might wonder whether a person can know the right course of action but still ask, "Why should *I* do it?" A failure to act in accordance with moral duty might arise not because of a failure to see the right action, nor because the desire to take this action is weaker than some contrary desire, but simply because of a lack of desire or motivation to do what is right.

Is this an instance of bad thinking? It depends. The problem of the relationship between moral reasoning and moral motivation is complex, and philosophers are generally of two minds on this issue. The question is essentially whether moral judgment—a reasoned and justified belief about what is right—is sufficient by itself to motivate a person to do the right thing (even if she happens not to end up actually doing it), or whether something else is needed beside belief—for example, a desire, appetite, feeling, or passion.

Some philosophers insist that cognitive states, like beliefs, are one thing, and motivational states—the things that move us to do what we do, to act on those beliefs—are another. Motivation, in other words, is in this view "external" to belief or judgment. No matter how much thinking you do, no matter how clearly and distinctly you perceive that a particular course of action is the right thing to do, it will not be enough to motivate you to perform the action. For "externalists," motivation requires something beyond cognition, something in addition to rational insight about the right and good. If you see a person drowning in a lake, you may (from the perspective of reason) perfectly well understand that saving that person is morally right. But the externalist insists that such understanding by itself will not move you to save the person unless it is supplemented by, say, a love or sympathy for the victim, a desire for the admiration of others, or the hope for reward.[31]

The eighteenth-century Scottish philosopher David Hume (1711–76), for one, argued that belief alone—that the action is right, that it is in your own best interest, or that it will increase happiness in the world—is not sufficient to arouse a person to action. Without a "sentiment of pleasure or disgust" or some other kind of feeling of approval or disapproval, the judgment of reason cannot cause you to do anything. "[Something] must touch the heart," Hume says; otherwise, you will remain unmoved, no matter what reason says.[32]

Other philosophers argue that a rational judgment that an action is right cannot *but* move one to perform the action. In this view, motivation is "internal" to moral reasoning. A belief about what is good or right is itself motivational; it is essentially and necessarily accompanied by the desire or inclination to so act, even if, for some reason—perhaps a strong countervailing passion or desire—the person does not end up executing the action.[33] If you have come to the conclusion that keeping a promise to a friend is the morally right thing to do, then, "internalists" insist, you must be motivated to some degree to keep that promise. You cannot then ask, "Why should I do it?," since in judging that it is right to keep the promise you *must* necessarily feel moved to do it—that is what judging something to be right involves (although it is still possible that you do not, in the end, keep the promise).[34]

What this means, though, is that if you think that an action is the right thing to do but still do *not* have any motivation to do it (and for that reason fail to do it), then in some way or another you have not in fact reasoned well. Something must have gone wrong in your thinking and judgment, such that you do not *really* see that the action is morally right. If you can still ask, "Why should I do it?," then, according to internalism, you must not really be seeing that it is the right thing to do. For the internalist, to know the good may not imply that one actually does the good—the best intentions do not always issue in successful action—but it does imply that you *want* to do the good. Thus, if you do *not* want to do the good—if you have no desire to save the drowning person—then you must not really be seeing what is good.

The debate between externalists and internalists, like so many philosophical debates, continues apace. In this case, a good deal may rest on some basic psychological, phenomenological and even neurobiological evidence. Are the internalists correct to say that you cannot see what is right without feeling some motivational pull toward doing it? Or are the externalists correct when they insist that, as a matter of introspective fact, you can have a strong and justified belief about the moral quality of an action without any desire or urge to do it?[35] Can you really believe that you ought to, say, call your parents if you feel no motivation to do so?

Relevant for our purpose, however, is the idea that a failure to act rightly can be the result of bad reasoning, of a failure to truly assess a situation and its moral character. When we go wrong in our action—whether we want to do the right thing but end up acting otherwise, or perceive the right thing to do but lack any motivation to do it—it is not necessarily because we are monsters or lack a moral sense or have perverse desires. It may simply be because we have gone wrong in our thinking and have not formed the proper beliefs about right and wrong or about the action at hand.[36]

How Responsible Are We?

We generally want other people to do the right thing. And for the most part we want to do the right thing ourselves. It does not require an unreasonably optimistic view of human nature to say that—again, for the most part—we strive to act according to our better moral judgment. We are not always successful in this endeavor, of course, but we usually feel bad when we do not act rightly. The pangs of conscience, sentiments of regret, even feelings of shame and embarrassment are natural when good people fail to follow their moral intuitions. This is especially the case when we recognize that it did not have to be that way—that we could in fact have acted otherwise and in conformity to our better beliefs and values. (Aristotle says that this is an important difference between the incontinent person and the intemperate person. Incontinent or weak people act contrary to their better judgment and so feel regret when they realize what they have done. Intemperate people, on the other hand, do not regret their bad action; they did precisely what they wanted to do. This, he says, is why intemperance is worse than incontinence.)[37]

Are we blameworthy when we fail to act rightly because of bad thinking, even when that bad thinking is not deliberate? Is a person to be held culpable either for not exercising judgment at all or for doing so but doing it poorly? Generally, yes. As rational moral agents, it is incumbent upon us to exercise our rationality and to do it well. But it really depends on how responsible we are for the bad thinking itself—that is, how responsible we are for missing information that would have led us to do what is right or for any poor reasoning that brought us to the wrong practical conclusions.

Sometimes we are willing to excuse people on the grounds that they could not have known better. This is true especially with children but occasionally also for adults. Often we will say that there are some things that individual people just could not have been expected to know. But *should* they, in fact, have known better? What is the explanation for their ignorance or inattention or poor reasoning? Did they lack crucial information for forming proper beliefs about right and wrong, or for drawing the proper conclusion about the correct action to take? If this information were unavailable or extremely difficult to acquire, then we are not likely to blame individuals for their subsequent wrongdoing. Smoking is now considered a classic example of *akrasia*. Smokers today know that what they are doing is bad for them, but they do it anyway. However, before medical research established that there was a connection between smoking and respiratory and other diseases, perhaps we might be reluctant to say that smokers were acting contrary to their better judgment.

But what if the ignorance or faulty reasoning was something entirely within their control? The individuals may have been *directly* negligent in their epistemic, and thus moral, agency. Perhaps, for some reason or other, they stubbornly refused to take account of some essential and easily accessible information. This was the case with the shipowner we discussed earlier, who permitted his ship to set sail with a full load of passengers either despite knowing of its perilous condition or, just as bad, refusing to look closely enough to see if the ship was seaworthy (because he knew what he might discover). The shipowner should have known his action was wrong, but he allowed greed to overwhelm both his epistemic responsibility and his moral sense. In other cases, people may find the evidence that is relevant to their moral decisions emotionally difficult to accept—say, an unexpected and uncomfortable truth about a person they love. Maybe some parents of children with autism are in such a situation. Their heartache drives them to ignore evidence that vaccines are not to blame and to advocate for policies that will only end up harming other children.

Of course, sometimes the poor choices that we make are due to nothing but laziness or impatience. We can be too casual or hasty in our reasoning and thus fail to draw the right conclusion about what to do. This may, in the end, be the best explanation for the examples of normative stubbornness we considered earlier. Why did the Madison School Board wrongly discipline the security officer who mentioned (but did not use) the racial slur? Why did the race officials callously disqualify the athlete who wore a hijab? And why did the store manager refuse to sell alcohol to the septuagenarian? In all of these cases, the poor judgments on display might be rooted in simple expediency. Deliberating about the right thing to do is just too much trouble.

Chapter 5

Wisdom

The youth of Athens loved to watch Socrates make self-important people squirm. He relentlessly questioned his fellow citizens, including politicians, physicians, and generals. He pressed and baited them until they conceded his point or fled in frustration and embarrassment. He implored them to reorder their priorities and give more care to character and the condition of the soul than to such ephemeral goods as wealth, power, and honor. Above all, he urged them, examine yourselves, for this is where a good human life begins. Take a close look at who you are and how you live. What, after all, do you really know? What do you value? Are you truly virtuous and, consequently, truly flourishing?

These, Socrates believed, are the most important questions of all.[1] They are also exceedingly difficult to answer, even though the object of investigation—oneself—is close at hand. However, Socrates insisted, the person who fails even to ask them lacks an essential component of a fully human life, and for this he should be ashamed. As Socrates proclaimed in one of the most famous and eloquent maxims in the history of philosophy, "the unexamined life is not worth living for a human being." And he, for one, never hesitated to let someone know when he was living a less than worthy life. Is it any wonder the citizens of Athens ordered his execution by poison?

———

In previous chapters, we looked at ways in which thinking can go badly wrong—through epistemic stubbornness of holding beliefs that have little to no justification or that actually fly in the face of overwhelming counter-evidence, and through various forms of fallacious argument. We considered remedies for these lapses in rationality in the laws of logic and principles of justification and reasoning. Attention to some basic and well-established rules is necessary in order to adopt and abandon beliefs in a responsible way.

We have also seen how what we have been calling "bad thinking" is not just an epistemic matter but can have serious moral consequences. A person who is not thinking well is, through a failure to exercise (and follow through on) good judgment, unlikely to act well and do the right thing. A parent who turns a blind eye to evidence that affirms the safety of vaccinations jeopardizes the lives of her children as well as of others. A school board that enforces its rules inflexibly and without proper discretion can cause its employees great distress and lead to unjust outcomes.

We would now like to step back in these final two chapters and look at the bigger picture. There is a broader, more vital context for the discussion of epistemic and moral rationality in the previous chapters. What, you may be wondering, do these apparently technical lessons of philosophy have to do with those most important questions that exercised Socrates and so annoyed his fellow Athenians—questions that have always been at the heart of philosophy: How should you live? What is human flourishing (*eudaimonia*), and how can you achieve it?

In fact, bad thinking is about more than just the particular beliefs you come to hold, the individual choices you make, and singular actions you undertake. At stake here is not just what you think and what you do, but the kind of person you are and the kind of life you lead. Good thinking and good judgment inform and make possible a "good life." Philosophy can save us from ourselves not only by keeping us from unjustified beliefs and thoughtless actions, but by actually putting us on the path to what Spinoza, for one, called "the right way of living."

The Virtue of Wisdom

The ancient Greeks before Socrates fully appreciated the importance of the character trait they called *sophia*, "wisdom." Among virtues, it typically reigned supreme. While they may have disagreed over what exactly wisdom is and how to acquire it, they all knew that without wisdom you could not live well. A lack of wisdom leads to unhappiness, even disaster. It is the stuff of tragedy.

There were even *philosophoi*, "lovers of wisdom," before Socrates. But when Socrates transformed philosophy from an investigation of the heavens and the world around us to an inquiry into the good life, from cosmology and natural science to ethics, he transformed the nature of wisdom itself. The wise person would no longer be simply someone who excelled at a specialized skill or even had a broad knowledge of things. Wisdom went beyond practical know-how, wealth of experience, and erudition. For Socrates, to be wise meant knowing how to live a rational life, and thus how to flourish as a human being.

And yet, despite its venerable history, wisdom may be the forgotten virtue. We seem to have lost touch with the one thing that, for centuries, was thought to make life worth living. If talk of wisdom comes up at all, it is typically in a religious context or in relation to some opaque notions of spirituality. There was a long period when even philosophers rarely talked much about the virtue that gives their vocation its very name.[2]

Most of us know—or think we know—what honesty, generosity, and benevolence are. We commonly use words like 'loyal,' 'humble,' and 'kind' to describe people, and we seem to have little trouble in identifying tolerant, charitable, and prudent behavior. Even justice, courage, and temperance, three of Plato's cardinal virtues, while somewhat more of a challenge to define, are nonetheless relatively familiar. They remain a central part of our ethical, social, and political vocabulary. We seek justice, admire courage, and pity or blame the intemperate person. We continue to pay homage to all these virtues, both in our words and, one hopes, in our deeds. They inform the way we think about people, practices, and institutions. They influence, however tacitly—and, again, one can only hope—our decisions and choices. They are the foundations of some of the most important judgments we make.

Wisdom is the fourth cardinal virtue, no less important—and perhaps even more so—than the others. (In one ancient view, all the virtues are simply forms of wisdom, applications of wisdom to different kinds of circumstances. Thus, courage would be wisdom exercised in the context of combat; temperance would be wisdom with respect to the enjoyment of bodily pleasures, and so on.) But we use the word 'wise' less frequently and more carelessly than 'just,' 'courageous,' and even 'temperate.' It seems to reek of antiquity and obsolescence. Wisdom is dusty. It belongs to the ages, if not the aged.

We do still speak of wise sayings, wise choices, even lives led wisely. There are wise men and wise women who do wise things and give wise advice to those who seek them out or buy their

books or listen to their podcasts. And philosophers, the devoted lovers of wisdom, continue to investigate matters moral
and metaphysical (although the practice of philosophy is now,
and has been for a long time, an academic profession rather
than a life's calling). But our cavalier way of tossing about the
word 'wise' to cover a disparate variety of things suggests that
we really do not have a shared and precise idea of what wisdom
is, and that we even lack articulate and defensible beliefs about
what it is to *be* wise. The wise person is not simply a witty, very
smart, or learned person. Wisdom is different from being a
quick study or knowing a lot, even if what is known is highly
important. As the philosopher Robert Nozick explains, "wisdom is not just knowing fundamental truths."[3] But what, then,
are we praising a person for when we consider her wise? And
why is wisdom, despite appearances, still relevant?

Part of the difficulty in answering these questions lies in the
apparent opacity of wisdom. Unlike the other Platonic virtues,
a person's wisdom is not so readily apprehended in observable
behavior. Courage and benevolence are unmistakably mani-
fested in, even defined by, the ways we act. Courage determines
how a person faces danger, whether she stands her ground or
retreats. The courageous person is seen to behave in certain
characteristic and appropriate ways, and we judge her courage
on the basis of that behavior. Benevolence is easily recognized
in how we deal with other people. The benevolent person treats
acquaintances and strangers with kindness and consideration
and shows respect for their dignity. Even temperance, and especially its corresponding vice, gluttony, is revealed in the way
in which one manages the appetites. The temperate person par-
takes of food, drink, and sexual pleasure in a disciplined manner, consuming neither too much nor too little. All of these
virtues, then, are fairly observable and public; they are moral or

social virtues. It thus seems easy enough to understand them—at least initially—in terms of the behavior with which they are associated.

It is tempting, by contrast, to think of wisdom as a more private affair. While wisdom can certainly manifest itself in what we say or do, we commonly view it as belonging primarily to one's inner life, something that is at work and is of value whether or not it ever results in outward behavior. According to this view, wisdom would be an intellectual virtue rather than a moral one. The hackneyed caricature of the wise man who sits on a mountaintop, alone with his thoughts and untroubled by any social intercourse or pragmatic challenges—except for those times when he is sought out by weary pilgrims—captures a popular image of wisdom. Unlike courage or charity, wisdom, in this way of thinking, would be defined as a state of mind, not a tendency to act in certain ways. There may be modes of behavior that we expect from a wise person—there are things we would be very surprised to see such a person do or hear her say—but wisdom would not be characterized in terms of those behaviors. This may be why we find it hard to say what exactly a wise action is or why wisdom should lead to this or that deed or utterance. A person's wisdom is hidden from view—or so it might seem.

However, writers of various sorts—philosophical, religious, literary—have known all along, and anyone who has given any thought to the matter would agree, that this is the wrong way to think of wisdom. A "wisdom" that lies fallow in the mind, issuing no directions for living, is hardly worthy of the name. Unlike the person operating under the influence of bad thinking, the wise person will be someone who is reasonable both in thought *and* in action.

It should now be clear where all this is heading. For if philosophy is going to save us—if, as we have said, it is to turn us away from bad thinking and the conduct to which those unfortunate habits of mind invariably lead and bring us to a better kind of life—it will be because philosophy, through those epistemological and moral lessons, is the purveyor of wisdom; and without wisdom—that is, wisdom proper, a cultivated skill set of reasonableness in both thought and action—one cannot live well.

Wisdom in Thought and in Practice

A wise person is someone who exercises good thinking in her opinions. She knows how to come to her beliefs in a rational way, and she does not hold on to those beliefs beyond the point when the evidence counts against them. She has internalized the lessons regarding justification and good reasoning that we have examined. This is wisdom's epistemic side. But if her condition is truly to count as wisdom, it must also be a source of guidance in what she does. The wise person thus also exercises good judgment in her deeds and projects. Presumably, wisdom would have prevented the school board from disciplining a security officer for mentioning a racial slur, the store owner from refusing to sell alcohol to an elderly customer, and the authorities from disqualifying the young athlete who wore a hijab.

Wisdom, in other words, is not just knowledge. As the philosopher John Kekes notes, "The possession of wisdom shows itself in reliable, sound, reasonable, in a word, good judgment. In good judgment, a person brings his knowledge to bear on his actions. To understand wisdom, we have to understand its connection with knowledge, action and judgment."[4] The wise person does what is right because she sees that it is right and desires to do it (at least in part) for just that reason. She rarely, if ever, allows the temptation of immediate gratification, passion, or other enticements to overrule her correct practical thinking. For these reasons, we most certainly *can* judge a person's wisdom—like her courage or temperance—on the basis of her behavior. Surely we would hesitate to call a person "wise" if we found her to be living a corrupt, dissolute, or sterile life.

We owe this conception of wisdom as a kind of epistemic and practical excellence, as a guide to good thinking and a particular way of living well, grounded in a secure knowledge of oneself, to the ancient philosophers—and to Socrates above all others. However, it took many generations for this highly personal, Socratic understanding of wisdom to emerge from earlier, more basic (not to mention more violent and heroic) Homeric beginnings. It is a long story but one worth reviewing.

Profiles in Wisdom

In his account of the Greek and Persian wars in the first half of the fifth century BCE, the ancient historian Herodotus tells the story of Oebares, squire to the Persian king Darius. After the death of King Cambyses, the Persian throne was empty and without any line of succession, legitimate or otherwise. This gives the Persians the opportunity to debate which political arrangement would be best. Should they anoint another king? Or should they opt for a new form of government—democracy, perhaps? Or oligarchy?

Darius, a member of a group of nobles charged with coming up with a plan, argues for monarchy: "One ruler, it is impossible to improve upon that, provided he is the best. His judgment will be in keeping with his character; his control of the people will be beyond reproach; his measures against enemies and traitors will be kept secret more easily than under other forms of government."⁵ The other members of the group agree.

But now the question turns to whom, from among this elite group, kingship should be granted. They need a fair and impartial process and decide to let nature make the choice for them. At dawn the next day they plan to mount their horses on the outskirts of the city. The crown would go to the one whose horse neighed first as the sun inched over the horizon. Darius, however, wants terribly to be king and is not content to leave it up to luck.

Now, Herodotus tells us, "Darius had a clever groom called Oebares." Darius goes to Oebares and tells him about the method agreed upon for choosing the next king and asks him to find a way to ensure that the prize would be his. "Well, master," the squire replies, "if your chance of winning the throne depends upon nothing but that, you may set you mind at rest. . . . I know a charm that will just suit our purpose." Oebares goes to the stables and finds a mare that he knows Darius's horse is particularly fond of, takes her to the outskirts of the city, and ties her up. He then walks Darius's horse around the mare several times, finally allowing him to mount her. The next morning, when it is time for the members of the group to line up on their horses and wait for the sunrise, Oebares first goes to the stables and rubs his hand on the mare's genitals. He keeps his hand in his pocket until the sun is just about to come up. Then, as the sun rises, he puts his hand right under the nose of Darius's horse. The horse snorts and neighs at the smell of his mate, and Darius wins the royal prize.

Herodotus says that Oebares is (according to one translation) "clever." The Greek word he uses is *sophos*. It means "wise" but not necessarily wise in a general, all-purpose way. You would not consult Oebares for guidance on how to live your life. The earliest uses of *sophos* and *sophia* in ancient Greek literature, in fact, have a rather restricted meaning. The word does suggest a kind of expertise and competence, and a *sophos* person will be someone you can rely on (much as Darius relies on Oebares). But his expertise is narrow, and he is to be relied on only in a specific domain. To be *sophos* in this early sense of the term is simply to be skilled in a particular craft or art (including, apparently, the art of deception).

A craft—what the ancient Greeks called *techné*—is any creative or productive activity that is guided by knowledge and understanding. Being skilled in a craft is not just having the knowledge but also being able to exercise that knowledge in making or doing.

Homer's Bronze Age world is filled with men and women who embody this sort of wisdom. Achilles, the Greek hero of the *Iliad*, is *sophos* in the art of war. Skamandrios, a Trojan warrior, is "a man of wisdom in the chase"; schooled by Artemis, the goddess of hunting, he is expert in "striking down every wild thing that grows in the mountain forest" with his bow and arrow.[6] Penelope, whose twenty-year wait for her husband Odysseus's return from war and wandering is portrayed in the *Odyssey*, must exercise intelligence, wit, and skill in fending off the many violent suitors who are pressing hard upon her.

Our reluctance to accept such mere craft-skill or even cleverness as true wisdom can probably be explained by the fact that we have inherited a rather different conception of wisdom, one that promises something more. This is nicely captured by something Aristotle says: "The term 'wisdom' is employed in the crafts to describe those who have the most exact expertise in the crafts, e.g., we call Pheidias a wise stone-worker and Polycleitus a wise bronze-worker, signifying nothing else by wisdom than excellence in a craft. But we also think some people are wise in general, not wise in some area."[7] Most of us today would instinctively agree with Aristotle on this. If we do think of wisdom, we tend to think of a much broader kind of virtue than craft-skill. The wise person, we might insist, has a more general capacity. He is skilled not just in one art or another, nor is his gift a kind of ingenuity or cunning. Rather, his virtue is reliable in an all-purpose way. His understanding and competence is not confined to archery, medicine, machines, or equine sexuality, but to life in general. He is qualified not just to lead an army or even a government, but to lead human beings in living. The wise person, we believe, is someone who has a grasp of the rules of living well and to whom we would turn when we want or need to know what to do.

Aristotle sees himself as speaking on this matter not only for his contemporaries but for history. He is referring to another conception of wisdom, one that was current well before his era (the fourth century BCE) and, like the first conception of wisdom, goes back to the time in which Homer's stories take place, the Archaic period of great kings and warriors. This wisdom is the kind of understanding of things human and natural that comes from a lifetime of experience. The longer the life, the more the wise person has seen and learned. Homer, for example, gives us "aged Nestor":

> In his time two generations of mortal men had perished,
> those who had grown up with him and they who had
>   been born to
> these in sacred Pylos, and he was king in the third age.[8]

The oldest of the Greek warriors at Troy, Nestor is still proud and formidable in battle. But his real contribution to the cause is the wealth of wisdom he offers his comrades. Over the course of a long life he has accumulated much knowledge. It is not so much a knowledge of facts as a knowledge of lessons. Nestor knows through his considerable experience how to get by, and even succeed, in the world. His sensible and practical counsels represent a kind of commonsense wisdom honed over a long period of time. He tells mighty Achilles that he should show more respect for Agamemnon, who, despite having seized Achilles's concubine as his own, is still the greater king and leader of the Greek invasion. And Nestor, "the aged man . . . whose advice had shown best before," tells Agamemnon how to rally his troops. Because of his long experience, Nestor knows a lot about war and other matters—at one point Homer calls him "wise in fighting from of old"—but he especially understands the hearts of men.

As great as Nestor may have been, there may be no better example of this type of wisdom than Solon—a man whose name has in fact become synonymous with wisdom. Solon was an Athenian poet and statesman of the late seventh and early sixth century BCE. At one point a political leader of Athens, he drafted for the city-state a constitution that, he hoped, would end the factional disputes that so divided the great democracy. He was a widely traveled man, and through his voyages he acquired a great knowledge of human nature and the ways of the world. The ancients counted him among the famed "Seven Wise Men."[9] His advice was sought not just in politics but also in moral matters and on the all-important question of the good life.

One time Solon was visiting Sardis, the capital of the Lydian Empire. Its emperor, Croesus, heard that the famous Greek legislator had arrived and sought him out to ask him some questions. According to Herodotus, Croesus gives his visitor a tour of the court and shows off his great wealth and power, "the richness and magnificence of everything." He then gets right to the point: "Well, my Athenian friend, I have heard a great deal about your wisdom, and how widely you have travelled in the pursuit of knowledge. I cannot resist my desire to ask you a question: who is the happiest man you have ever seen?"[10]

The answer that Solon gives is not the one Croesus was hoping to hear. Solon tells him of some very ordinary people who lived with great honor and died enviable deaths. Not only does Croesus miss top honors, he does not even make the list. Angry with Solon, he presses him: "That's all very well, my Athenian friend; but what of my own happiness? Is it so utterly contempt-ible that you won't even compare me with mere common folk like those you have mentioned?" Solon now clarifies the lesson that the emperor had failed to derive on his own. "The total days of [a human life] of seventy years is 26,250, and not a single one of them is like the next in what it brings. You can see from that, Croesus, what a chancy thing life is. You are very rich, and you rule numerous people; but the question you asked me I will not answer, until I know that you have died happily. Great wealth can make a man no happier than moderate means, unless he has the luck to continue in prosperity to the end." There are many ingre-dients in a happy life, Solon continues: "sound body, health, free-dom from trouble, fine children, good looks," not to mention sufficient means to satisfy the basic appetites. Moreover, it does not hurt to have good luck. "No man is self-sufficient," he warns Croesus; "there is sure to be something missing. But whoever has the greatest number of these good things, and keeps them to the end, and dies a peaceful death, that man, my lord Croesus, de-serves in my opinion to be called happy." If Solon has learned anything from a lifetime's experience, it is this: judge no one to have led a happy life until the day he or she has died.

Expertise in a particular craft, the natural fruit of long experi-ence, even (according to some ancient accounts) a supernatural gift in the form of divination—to the pre-Socratic mind *sophia* could mean any or all of these things. It is always a kind of knowledge. But it is one thing to say that such knowledge is the comprehension of the rules of some productive art, another to say that it is an understanding of the ways of the world and of human nature that comes after years of eventful living, and yet another to view it as the ability to read omens and discern the minds of the immortals.

But what about the philosopher—the lover of *sophia*? How does he fit into this picture? Whatever philosophy is, the object of its desire is surely not mere technical craft-skill, clever advice, or the gift of divine inspiration.

Lovers of Wisdom

The very first philosophers in ancient Greece, like Socrates and Plato after them, had great contempt for poets like Homer, Hesiod, and Pindar. It is not that the philosophers did not enjoy being entertained by epic, pastoral, and lyric poems. However, by virtue of their talents in the craft of poetry and its wide range of subject matters—war, nature, politics, gender relations, and, not the least, the gods—the ancient poets set themselves up as all-purpose teachers. As the great comic dramatist Aristophanes, in his play *The Frogs*, has one character say, "From the very earliest times the really great poet has been the one who had a useful lesson to teach." (In the play, the salvation of the city of Athens will come from one of the tragic poets. The only question, then, is: which one, Aeschylus or Euripides?)

Xenophanes, a thinker from the sixth century BCE, concedes that "from the beginning all people have learned from Homer." He insists, however, that what they got from the great bard was nothing but disinformation and lies. The poets, he claims—and he means to include the writers of both epic and dramatic literature—"misrepresent the gods" and portray them as engaged in activities that are "blameworthy and shameful among men: stealing, committing adultery, and deceiving each other."[11] Worthless anthropomorphisms, Xenophanes complains.

Likewise, Heraclitus, the philosopher famous for claiming that all is in flux and change, and therefore "no one steps into the same river twice, because it is not the same river and he is not the same man," accuses the poets of making the most elementary mistakes, such as not knowing the nature of night and day. He argues that the poets may have learned many things, but they lack true understanding.[12]

These earliest philosophers were wedded to an altogether different conception of wisdom from that which ruled the popular and poetic imagination. The philosopher's wisdom, while it may involve an understanding of the gods and the demands of piety, is not a matter of craft know-how or long and rich experience. For Xenophanes, Heraclitus, Thales, Anaxagoras, Anaximander, and others, wisdom is scientific understanding of the world, and it is acquired through directed inquiry and thoughtful reflection on the nature of things.

Thus, Thales, a man so consumed by his investigations that he reportedly once fell into a well because he was gazing at the sky, says that everything is, at the most fundamental level, water. Whatever is, is water in one form or another. Anaximenes says no, not water but air is the ultimate building block of nature; everything, whether it is a solid, a liquid, or a gas, is constituted by air. Heraclitus agrees that there is some single stuff from which everything is made, but he insists that it is neither water nor air but fire. The great variety of things in the world are all manifestations of fire, either the condensation or rarefication of that most elementary matter. Finally, the ecumenical Empedocles claims that there are in fact four basic principles of nature—earth, air, fire, and water—and that the generation and disintegration of things comes about as these elements are combined and separated by the forces of Love and Strife.

Despite this diversity of opinion, there is something that Thales, Anaximenes, Heraclitus, and Empedocles share. Socrates tells us what this is in Plato's dialogue *Phaedo*, when he recalls for his companion Cebes his own youthful ardor for a certain type of inquiry. "When I was young, Cebes, I had an extraordinary passion for that branch of learning which is called natural science. I thought it would be marvelous to know the causes for which each thing comes and ceases and continues to be. I was constantly veering to and fro, puzzling primarily over this sort of question. Is it when heat and cold produce fermentation, as some have said, that living creatures are bred? Is it with the blood that we think, or with the air or the fire that is in us? . . . Then again, I would study celestial and terrestrial phenomena, until at last I came to the conclusion that I was uniquely unfitted for this form of inquiry."[13] The young Socrates, before turning to what would be his true philosophical mission, the quest for human goodness, apparently went through a period in which he, too, wanted to know about the principles of things. Like Thales and the others, he sought an understanding of nature. But the early philosophers were after not just a collection of facts. They did not want to know simply that fire is ubiquitous and that it is hot and burns, or that water corrodes iron and freezes at a certain temperature, or that the stars move across the sky from east to west, and so on. No mere compendium of natural phenomena, no matter how complete, would count as "understanding." Something more was needed, something the Greeks called a *logos*.

The term *logos* can mean "word," "language," or "speech," but it can also mean "story" or "narrative." Sometimes, when the story is provided in order to make clear *why* something happened as it did, *logos* can mean "explanation" or "reason" or "cause." If you should ask why fire burns and water freezes, an explanation will take the form of a story about heat, molecules, and thermodynamics. These will be essential ingredients in the *logos* of the phenomenon.

Lovers of wisdom—a new kind of wisdom that brings us closer to what Socrates had in mind—Thales of Milesia, Anax-imenes of Eurystratus, and Heraclitus, son of Bloson of Ephe-seus, all sought a *logos*. They wanted to discover an account of all things and an explanation for why they are as they are. The task of philosophy, as they saw it, was to arrive at a relatively simple, systematic, and comprehensive story that reduces na-ture's complex and rich phenomena to its most basic elements. By appealing to a few irreducible principles—water or air or fire or all four elements, plus a few dynamic forces of attraction or repulsion—the philosopher's account should explain every-thing that is. Even today, many philosophers would approve of this conception of the philosopher's job. In the words of Wilfrid Sellars (1912–89), "The aim of philosophy, abstractly formu-lated, is to understand how things in the broadest sense of the term hang together in the broadest sense of the term."[14]

A worthwhile account moves from the visible and superficial diversity and variety of things to their hidden unity. It allows one deeply to understand nature by revealing the sources of its order. A person with such an account will know nature's most primary constituents—the building blocks from which every-thing is made—and its governing laws. He will know what *kinds* of stuff there are, how different things are manifestations of those fundamental materials, and why they behave as they do. As Heraclitus announces at the beginning of his work, "all things happen according to this *logos* . . . [wherein] I distinguish each thing according to its constitution and declare how it is."[15]

In short, a *logos* was supposed to do exactly what we still envision a scientific theory doing: provide a complete explanation of everything in as few terms as possible. Today, it is a small number of kinds of subatomic components (particles, "strings") and the workings of a short list of forces (gravity, electromagnetism, and strong and weak forces); in 500 BCE, it was (at least according to Empedocles) the four elements and the powers of Love and Strife.

Western philosophy is often said to have begun with a certain wonder about the world. This is true enough. But rather than resorting to a mythopoetic explanation of what and how and why—such as a primordial creation story and the inscrutable and unpredictable activity of divinities—the first philosophers appealed to the lawlike causal behavior of empirically familiar items (water, air, love).[16] Moreover, philosophy made its case roughly through observation, theorizing, and reasoning rather than through dogmatic assertion or the invocation of some authority (Zeus, Homer). Above all, a proper *logos* would be a comprehensive, unifying theory of, to quote Xenophanes, "all things."[17]

In an ancient philosophical system, there may still be gods playing an active role in the world. And maybe only the gods truly know how it all hangs together. The philosophers before Socrates did not completely abandon the mythological or religious elements that color the tales of the poets. Heraclitus believed that there is a wisdom or intelligence governing the cosmos, and he called it "Zeus." Nonetheless, even if there are higher beings ultimately in charge, the natures of things and the powers that immediately direct them are, at least in principle, scrutable. To comprehend them, along with the teleological principles that govern the cosmos, is wisdom. The wise person understands the natural and divine worlds. "Wisdom is one thing," Heraclitus says, "to understand the intelligence that controls all things through all things."[18]

Socrates agreed with his Milesian and Ionian predecessors that wisdom and philosophy are connected with providing a *logos*. But he thought that their efforts were misdirected. According to Xenophon, who, like Plato, knew Socrates personally, their mentor "did not discuss that topic so favored by other talkers, the nature of the universe, and avoided speculation on the so-called cosmos of the professors, how it works, and on the laws that govern the phenomena of the heavens. Indeed, he would argue that to trouble one's mind with such problems is sheer folly."[19] This may seem an odd position for a philosopher to take. And yet, Socrates reportedly insisted, these kinds of inquiries do not in fact do what wisdom is supposed to do. "Did these thinkers suppose that their knowledge of human affairs was so complete that they must seek these new fields for the exercise of their brains; or that it was their duty to neglect human affairs and consider only things divine?"[20] What is this "knowledge of human affairs" that, for Socrates, constitutes the proper subject of philosophy? It is knowing what makes a human being good. Wisdom provides a person with a knowledge of himself and of the right way to live. As Nozick puts it, "wisdom is what you need to understand in order to live well and cope with the central problems and avoid the dangers in the predicaments human beings find themselves in." It is about "the guidance of life."[21]

For Socrates, a *logos* was still central to wisdom. However, the explanation or reason or account valued by the wise person was not sought in the workings of nature. The subject truly in need of a *logos* was one's own life.

Chapter 6

The Philosophical Life

Much of this book has been devoted to analysis and diagnosis. We have explained what bad thinking is and examined how and why it happens. We have shown, as well, that bad thinking is a matter not just of thought but of action. A failure to reason well affects what we do, and thus has moral consequences.

Beyond simply identifying a problem—and not just an abstract, "merely philosophical" problem but a very real and concrete one that has left way too many in America (and elsewhere) entertaining absurd beliefs and promoting dangerous policies—we are also offering a prescription. There is a way to avoid bad thinking. There are "best practices" when it comes to reasoning and judgment, and many of these are readily learned through philosophy, through the study of its history, problems, and methods.

Finally, to switch from a medical to a legal metaphor, we are also engaged in a bit of advocacy. This book represents a brief or plea for a certain kind of life. It is a life that, while first described and promoted in antiquity, remains today a life very much worth living. In fact, according to one renowned expert—who, it should be clear by now, is the hero of the book—it is the *only* life worth living.

There is no better way to sum up the epistemological and ethical points we have been making than to turn, at last, to Socrates's own conception of wisdom and his famous claim that the "unexamined life is not worth living." What exactly does he mean by an "examined life"? What does it take to lead such a life? Why is it the only life worth living? And what role do such virtues or habits as "wisdom" and "good thinking" play in an examined life?[1]

Knowing What You Are Doing

In Plato's dialogue *Euthyphro*, we find Socrates on the eve of the trial that will end in his conviction and execution. The official charges brought against him by some leading citizens of Athens are "failing to recognize the city's gods, introducing other new divinities, and breaking the law because he corrupts the youth of the city." However, Socrates knows—and we know—that the real reason for his indictment is the resentment and suspicion he has generated after years of harassing Athenians about the lives they were leading. Socrates has a bad reputation, in part because of those he calls the "old accusers"—people like Aristophanes, whose unflattering portrayal of Socrates in plays like *The Clouds* (produced in 423 BCE) only reinforced the animus against him.

As the dialogue opens, Socrates is preparing to face his accusers and answer the charges. On his way to court for a preliminary hearing, he encounters his friend Euthyphro, who is also occupied with a serious legal matter.

When Euthyphro's father discovered that one of his laborers had killed another man, he bound the killer "hand and foot" and threw him into a ditch while awaiting word from a priest on what to do. The laborer eventually died from exposure, and

Euthyphro is now prosecuting his father for murder. Socrates is taken aback by this news and asks the young man how he could do something so audacious as to charge his own father with a serious crime. Euthyphro, who claims to have "accurate knowledge of all such things," replies that "what I am doing is the pious thing to do, prosecuting a wrongdoer . . . whether the wrongdoer is your father or your mother or anyone else; not prosecuting is impious."[2] This, naturally, leads Socrates to wonder what Euthyphro means by "piety," and so the usual interrogation ensues.

The dialogue, like so many of Plato's works, seems to end on a disappointing note. While Socrates's conversation with Euthyphro is ostensibly about the nature of piety, they reach no conclusions on the subject. Euthyphro does make several attempts to explain the nature of piety, but Socrates refutes each with an effective *reductio ad absurdum*. This is a classical argumentative trope whereby you show (with the help of some self-evident and indisputable premises) that your opponent's thesis actually leads to an absurd or contradictory conclusion and therefore must be rejected. Thus, if, as Euthyphro says in his opening bid, something is pious because the gods love it; and if, as we know from Homer and other tales involving the Olympian deities, the gods often disagree about (and even fight over) what they love and what they hate, then one and the same thing can be loved by some gods and hated by others. From this it follows, in Euthyphro's definition of 'piety,' that one and the same thing would be both pious and impious, which is an absurdity. Euthyphro's starting assumption about piety must therefore be wrong.

Socrates himself never explains what, in his view, piety really is. When Euthyphro's third effort at refining his definition is unsuccessful, Socrates suggests that they give it another go.

Euthyphro, however, has had enough. He begs off with the excuse that he has more pressing things to take care of.

> SOCRATES: So we must investigate again from the
> beginning what piety is, as I shall not willingly give up
> before I learn this. . . . So tell me, my good Euthyphro,
> and do not hide what you think.
> EUTHYPHRO: Some other time, Socrates, for I am in a
> hurry now, and it is time for me to go.[3]

The failure of the two men to make any progress in defining piety, in explaining the essence of this virtue, indicates that, as important as such a topic is to these ancient Greeks, it may not be the real point of the dialogue.

Euthyphro is arrogant and stubborn, embodying all the callowness of youth. He thinks he knows when he does not. He is confident, even cocksure, that what he is doing is the right thing to do—confident that he *knows* that it is pious to prosecute his father—even though it turns out that his ideas about piety are ill-formed. It never occurs to him that his beliefs about piety—and by the end of the dialogue he seems not quite sure *what* he believes—might be either false, confused, or unwarranted. His muddled thoughts may indeed have led him to the correct belief about piety. But even if his belief *is* true, because he cannot coherently explain it, much less successfully defend it, the belief is unjustified, and so he does not actually *know* the true nature of piety.

Still, one might reasonably ask: "So what?" Euthyphro does not know, in the rigorous philosophical sense of 'know,' what piety is. But perhaps prosecuting his father for murder is indeed the right thing to do. And even if it is not, well, he has good intentions. What more do we want? To blame Euthyphro for his epistemic arrogance when the real concern is whether he is doing the right thing, or at least intending to do the right thing, looks like pedantry. Is it not enough that he at least thinks he is satisfying the demands of piety, and maybe even actually *is* satisfying these demands? If his intentions are good—and, moreover, if his action happens to be right—why should we care about whether Euthyphro's beliefs qualify, philosophically and technically, as *knowledge,* as opposed to what Socrates elsewhere calls "right opinion"?

In fact, the dialogue is not about the nature of piety at all. But neither is it a purely epistemological investigation into Euthyphro's ignorance and, more generally, the conditions for knowledge. This is clear from something that Socrates says at the beginning of the dialogue and that, to emphasize the point, he repeats right at the end. After learning why Euthyphro would do something so momentous and unfilial as prosecuting his own father, but before challenging Euthyphro to defend the piety of his action, Socrates says something that looks like a casual, throwaway line but actually represents the crucial philosophical point of the dialogue: "By Zeus, Euthyphro, you think that your knowledge of the divine, and of piety and impiety, is so accurate that, when those things happened as you say, you have no fear of having acted impiously in bringing your father to trial?"[4]

Socrates is offering Euthyphro a warning: "I hope you *know* what you are doing!," where the word 'know' should be understood in its strongest possible sense. Lest the reader not see the import of this remark, Socrates reiterates it, at greater length, at the very end of the dialogue, just before a frustrated Euthyphro scurries off.

> So we must investigate again from the beginning what piety is, as I shall not willingly give up before I learn this. Do not think me unworthy, but concentrate your attention and tell

the truth. For you know, if any man does, and I must not let you go, like Proteus,[5] before you tell me. *If you had no clear knowledge of piety and impiety you would never have ventured to prosecute your old father for murder on behalf of a servant. For fear of the gods you would have been afraid to take the risk lest you should not be acting rightly, and would have been ashamed before men,* but now I know well that you believe you have clear knowledge of piety and impiety. So tell me, my good Euthyphro, and do not hide what you think it is.[6]

Again, Socrates cautions his friend: I hope you *know* what you are doing—I hope that in undertaking to prosecute your father you are acting not simply on a hunch, a guess, a random opinion, an intuition, or even a firmly held belief about piety that, while possibly true, is not something you can defend with good reasons. He wants Euthyphro to see that acting on the basis of something less than knowledge—real knowledge—is a serious matter indeed.

In other words, the main point that Socrates is making in Plato's dialogue is a moral one. Bad thinking in the form of epistemic arrogance and stubbornness, persisting in beliefs that you cannot successfully defend or justify, is one thing. Relying on such flawed beliefs to guide your choice of action is quite another, and it will have serious practical and ethical consequences. One needs not just to *believe* that one is doing the right thing, but to *know* that one is doing the right thing. Socrates is here offering a succinct description of all the lessons we have tried to impart so far, from our discussion of Descartes's and Clifford's evidentialism, through Bacon's warnings about confirmation bias, to Aristotle's and Spinoza's analyses of the role discretion and judgment should play in guiding action.

We can put Socrates's admonition, which sets a very high bar for proper moral action, in the form of an argument:

1. In order to be acting piously—that is, acting in a pious way—one must know that the action one is performing is pious. (In other words, there is no "accidental" piety; one must know that one is acting piously.)
2. In order to know that the action one is performing is pious, one must know what piety is. (How else would one know that the action is the pious thing to do?)[7]
3. Therefore, in order to act piously, one must know what piety is.

If talk about "piety," an ostensibly religious concept, seems odd or antiquated, we can reframe the argument by substituting the moral notion of "right": In order to be acting rightly, you must know that your action is right; and in order to know that your action is right, you must know what rightness is, what makes something right. Euthyphro clearly lacks knowledge of piety (rightness); so even if he happens to be doing the pious (right) thing in prosecuting his father—and Socrates never really questions that—he is not *acting* in a pious (right) way. The course of action that he is pursuing may not be wrong, but he simply does not know *what* he is doing.

The extent of bad thinking, as we have seen in previous chapters, is expansive. It goes beyond thought itself and includes whether one is doing the right thing in the right way and for the right reasons. Euthyphro thinks he knows when he does not, and that is an unfortunate epistemic condition. But his first-order failure to know the nature of piety, compounded by his second-order failure to recognize that he does not know—a failure to have knowledge about his (lack of) knowledge—not to mention his ultimate refusal to remedy his deficient epistemic condition: all of this infects his actions as well. After all, Euthyphro is ultimately confident that he is doing the right thing. And maybe the action that he is performing *is* the right thing to do. But if he is performing the right action, he does so unwittingly. He is like a small child whose fingers just happen to strike the right keys on a piano to produce Beethoven's "Ode to Joy." Bad thinking leads to bad acting even when the action just happens to be good.

The lesson of this Socratic exercise is simple enough: think—think hard and think well—before you act. Make sure that you understand the reasons for your actions and that your confidence that you are doing the right thing is warranted. Good, practical advice, of course. It seems, in fact, just what common sense demands. Still, that is not all there is to the story. Socrates has even more to teach us about the how and why of good thinking before Athens forces the seventy-one-year-old philosopher to drink the cup of hemlock.

Defending Your Life

During his trial, as portrayed in another dialogue by Plato, the *Apology of Socrates*,[8] Socrates stands before his Athenian peers and defends his life as a philosopher. At the risk of angering the five hundred members of the jury even further and exacerbating his situation, he chides them for pursuing such things as wealth and honor instead of "more important goods" and for neglecting what is truly best. He reproves them for leading a certain kind of life. "My good friend, you are an Athenian and belong to a city which is the greatest and most famous in the world for its wisdom and strength. Are you not ashamed that you give your attention to acquiring as much money as possible, and similarly with reputation and honor, and give no attention or thought to truth and understanding and the perfection of your soul?"[9] Then comes the famous passage, offered in response to the suggestion that Socrates submit to exile instead of death:

> Perhaps someone might say: But Socrates, if you leave us [and go into exile] will you not be able to live quietly, without talking? Now this is the most difficult point on which to convince some of you. If I say that it is impossible for me to keep quiet because that means disobeying the god, you will not believe me and will think that I am being ironical. On the other hand, . . . I say that it is the greatest good for a man to discuss virtue every day and those other things about which you hear me conversing and testing myself and others, for *the unexamined life is not worth living for man*.[10]

The Greek term that Plato has Socrates use, *anexetastos bios*, which is often translated as "an unexamined life," is better rendered by the phrase "a life without examination." This captures the fact that such a life lacks a particular kind of *activity*.

Socrates's idea of "a life without examination" might seem easy enough to describe in a general way. It is the life of someone who never seriously questions things, least of all his own actions and plans. Such a person might indeed ask whether his actions or those of his friends or community or government are expedient, or popular, or even pleasant. But he does not, or only rarely, asks whether they are, in fact, *good*.

The unexamined life is a life of moral and intellectual passivity—which, for Socrates, are one and the same thing. The person leading this kind of life takes the world, including his own place therein, as it comes. He is content simply to do things as they have always been done *because* they have always been done that way and, just as important, because he enjoys them and sees no reason to change. He accepts the status quo and never subjects it to any kind of normative review. His life is one of conformity, an easy cycle of pleasures (and some pains) without critical inquiry and without serious reflection. No thought is given to unrealized possibilities, to how things might be better, or even just different. To sum it up in the form of a crude but effective image: the unexamined life is the life spent in front of the television watching junk and eating crap.

Now this might capture, fairly enough, Socrates's sense of a life "without examination." And yet, the description itself, like the life it depicts, seems rather superficial. Socrates must be telling us something more profound than simply to "question things" and not be so passive. If that is all he has in mind, the advice would be rather trite and anodyne: like the counsel to think before you act—good to know but hardly a deep philosophical insight.

Moreover, there seem to be obvious exceptions to this broad characterization of the unexamined life. There is no reason why the person leading the unexamined life must be a dull and passive conformist. The unexamined life can certainly be an exceptional life, a life of action and exploit. Achilles, for one, is a man of extreme emotions and bold conduct. He is special, and he knows it. He is the great hero of the Greek forces besieging Troy. He sees himself as standing well above his peers and not bound by the same rules as everyone else. The problem is, when he acts, he is led by passionate impulse rather than rational reflection. His ill-tempered (but, one might think, understandable) response to Agamemnon's seizing of his concubine, his brooding withdrawal from battle, even his decision to rejoin the fight (but only after his close companion Patroclus has been killed by the Trojan warrior Hector) all testify to the impetuous and temperamental—and unexamined—nature of his behavior. The unexamined life can be a life of quiet conformity, but it can also be a life of vaunted heroism and woeful tragedy.

Then there is the question of Socrates's meaning when he says that a life without examination is "not worth living." He surely does not mean that a person living an unexamined life should end it all. And he cannot be saying that society for the sake of its own improvement has the right to eliminate such people. No doubt Socrates wants to see more Athenians living an examined life, but this is not to be achieved through violence or ostracism. Socrates is a philosopher, not a social engineer; he is out to improve people, not punish them.

When Socrates tells the jury that an unexamined life is "not worth living," he means that those who neglect the relevant kind of examination are living a less than fully human life. A person is not exercising the distinctively human endowment to the degree he should, if he is even exercising it at all. If the human capacity for reason distinguishes us from other creatures, then a life without examination is a life in which a uniquely, essentially human characteristic is not put to use in the best way possible. It is like a thoroughbred race horse that spends its days in a stable. The unexamined life is not worth living because it falls short of the ideal life for the kind of rational being that we are.

But again, these sentiments might seem rather obvious. Stating in very general terms how an unexamined life falls short and why it leads to an imperfect existence is relatively easy. More challenging is to specify, in detail, the positive demands of the examined life—the philosophical life—and to explain how a person meets them only by exercising her rational capacities to the fullest. What *is* examination and how are you supposed to put it to work? And why should we think that such a life is better, more *worthy* of us, than any other kind of life?

As the case of Euthyphro shows, the most basic requirement of the examined life concerns action. Its focus is on the things we do and the projects we undertake. The call is not for specific kinds of action, however. Engaging in an examined life does not ask you (or forbid you) to do anything at all—other than engage in examination, of course. This is an important point. The examined life does not come with its own normative ethics. It does not entail any substantive moral principle—not even the Golden Rule—and does not present any particular pre-scriptions or proscriptions or issue any commands to do this or that. The imperative to live an examined life contains no inher-ent instructions about good and bad or right and wrong. Simply engaging in the requisite examination does not, by itself, tell you to follow the mean and avoid excess, exhort you to act only on a maxim that could become a universal law, or direct you to increase the general happiness. It does not even tell you what piety is. The examined life, in other words, is neutral with re-spect to concrete moral counsels. These have to do with the *content* of your life, whereas examination is about its *form*.

The most elementary demand of the examined life is not about actually performing any action at all. Rather, it is just the point that Socrates was trying to get across to Euthyphro, and it is not very different from what we were saying in earlier chap-ters about exercising judgment. It concerns the preconditions for action. As we saw, the lesson was a simple one: think hard and well enough before undertaking some course of action so that you *know* what you are doing, such that your confidence that you are doing the right thing is truly warranted. And bear in mind that "thinking hard" requires appreciation of just those canonical forms of good reasoning we have examined.

When he emphasizes the significance of the examined life, Socrates intends more than the glib aphorism that you must think before you act, and that good planning is the key to good action. Such truisms do not at all capture the substance and strength of the requirement. After all, doing "the right thing" might be just a practical counsel of prudential rationality: hav-ing chosen your goal, whatever it may be, make sure that you know the best means to achieve it. David Hume did not have a lot of confidence in reason, and he gave it a very limited domain of responsibility. In *A Treatise on Human Nature*, he says that "reason is and ought only to be the slave of the passions."[11] What he means is that practical reason is purely instrumental. It will not tell you what is good, what you ought to pursue, much less motivate you to pursue it; it will tell you only *how* to get what you want.

By contrast, the examined life is not about simply thinking ahead and having an efficacious plan of action for satisfying your desires. Even when equipped with the ability to reason in all the rationally ideal ways we discussed in earlier chapters, your actions may deviate from the demands of piety or rightness. Such an ability may lead you to the best strategy for achieving your end, but it will not tell you what the *best* end is. You may have some necessary tools for living an examined life, but they are not sufficient. Socrates's admonition to Euthyphro, when he expresses the hope that Euthyphro knows what he is doing, is that he ask himself a crucial question before undertaking so serious a thing as prosecuting his father for murder: In light of what I know about piety and justice, and considering the nature of the action I am about to perform, do I have good reasons for thinking that this is the pious and just thing to do?

In other words, the examined life begins—but only begins—with the examination of your actions from a reflective moral perspective. This is Socrates's primary warning to Euthyphro, and it bears repeating. It calls for the scrutiny of what you do in the light of your beliefs about ethical values. At this level, it does not really matter what those values or principles are or how you arrived at them. All that is required in this rudimentary version of the examined life is that before undertaking any meaningful action, you inquire into its moral quality. You must try to determine whether the action about to be performed is, under the circumstances and relative to your values, the right action and conducive to a good end. This is not a question to be taken lightly and addressed with some shallow intuition or feeling. It must be answered by appealing to your sincere beliefs about what is right and good to evaluate the character of the action. To do anything less is to act blindly.

You need to think about what you are doing, especially in momentous situations, and do so in a deep and reflective way. A person who is examining his actions in the proper manner is not just wondering haphazardly about whether the action will get him into trouble, or whether the project will be appreciated and praised (and maybe even rewarded) by others. His personal and idiosyncratic hopes and fears and inclinations are irrelevant. His history of achievements or plans for future accomplishments are of no concern. Only general principles about the right and the good should guide his decisions about how to act. As Socrates puts it before the jurors at his trial: "Someone might say 'Are you not ashamed, Socrates, to have followed the kind of occupation that has led to your being now in danger of death?' However, I should be right to reply to him: 'You are wrong, sir, if you think that a man who is any good at all should take into account the risk of life or death; he should look only to this in his actions, whether what he does is right or wrong, whether he is acting like a good or a bad man.'"[12] Only questions such as these will help a person do the right thing in the right way.

Now it might be argued that Euthyphro did at least this much when he decided to prosecute his father. After all, he claimed it was the pious thing to do, and so he must have engaged in *some* moral reflection on the nature of his action. However, this seems to be belied by the subsequent conversation. He cannot really answer Socrates's questions about the course he took. His remark about why prosecuting his father is the pious thing to do seems to come off the top of his head, and so it is doubtful whether he really examined his plan of action in a thoughtful way.

In other words, Socrates wants from Euthyphro—and from others—a *logos*. But while Thales, Heraclitus, and the other ancient *physikoi* (philosopher-scientists) sought an account of the world around them, a revelation of nature's underlying elements and principles, Socrates's objective lies closer to home. He wants an account of a person's behavior. This does not mean that he is interested in the physiological mechanisms of the human body's movements when a person does something. But neither does he really care about the psychological forces—such as passion, desire, or the will—that lead a person to do one thing rather than another. In the case of Euthyphro's prosecution, it is indeed useful and relevant to know that he is angry at his father for allowing a man to die. But what Socrates is after are not causes but *reasons*. The account that Socrates wants when he questions others about their actions is a rational one. The examined life requires of a person at this elementary stage that she be able to reveal the underlying principles of her actions—indeed, of her life. She must be able to articulate the reasons for the things she does. This, Socrates tells the jury after the guilty verdict has been pronounced upon him, is all that he was asking when he cross-examined his fellow citizens. "I say, gentlemen, to those who voted to kill me, that vengeance will come upon you immediately after my death, a vengeance much harder to bear than that which you took in killing me. You did this in the belief that you would avoid *giving an account of your life*, but I maintain that quite the opposite will happen to you. . . . You are wrong if you believe that by killing people you will prevent anyone from reproaching you for not living in the right way. To escape such tests is neither possible nor good."[13]

To provide an account of your life—of what you do and how you live—is to give a reason for it. An account of a life is supposed to justify it. In the 1991 film *Defending Your Life*, the characters played by Albert Brooks and Meryl Streep, having died, find themselves in a juridical limbo before moving on to their final and eternal destination. That destination will be determined by how well they explain themselves before their judges. That is, they are now called upon to give an account of their lives and argue for why they deserve to go to heaven.

In an examined life, this evaluative exercise does not take place only at the end of your allotted time, with a deathbed retrospective and accounting of how you lived. Rather, you are justifying yourself all along. Moreover, unlike the characters in the film, you are expected to engage in this kind of *apologia* not so much to others but especially to yourself. You do this by appealing to values and principles, to a conception of good and bad and right and wrong, that you find compelling. If asked by others to account for your actions, you are prepared to say *why* you chose to perform them, and to do so by explaining why, in your view, they were the right things to do. As Socrates says, "a person who is worth anything . . . has only one thing to consider in performing any action—that is, whether he is acting rightly or wrongly, like a good man or a bad man."

You may not be immediately aware of the general moral principles that move you to act as you do; you may not be entirely sure *what* you believe on matters of right and wrong and good and bad. Perhaps all your judgments about such things are underdeveloped, more intuitive than rational and hard to express as propositions. (The price of living an unexamined life is that you lose track of your most fundamental beliefs; you become morally unconscious.) And yet, to the extent that you are a rational and responsible moral agent—something you cannot help but be—you *must* have some beliefs in this regard. It may take prolonged reflection in order to determine and articulate your moral values and how you should use them to assess your actions. You might find that you are in fundamental agreement with the utilitarian philosophy that an action is right if it leads to an increase in the general happiness of all those affected by it. Or perhaps you accept Kant's principle that you have an absolute duty to act in such a way that you never treat other human beings merely as means to an end, as tools or instruments, but always show respect for their autonomy and dignity. Or maybe there is some other principle, or set of principles, that you find more persuasive. Part of the challenge of the moral life lies in the difficulty of identifying precisely which criteria to employ in grounding our choices and judgments.

Socrates has his own ideas about how one should go about resolving this deep perplexity about values and principles, and this will constitute a higher, second-order stage in the examined life. In the end, you will not be able to say for certain whether you are doing right or wrong until you have figured out the correct meaning of right and wrong, of good and bad. That is, you will have to be able to defend not only your actions in the light of your principles, but those principles themselves. At the elementary level we have been considering, though, where the setting of goals and their pursuit in action take place against the background of thought and reflection upon ethical standards, all that is being asked is that you step back from your practical engagements and raise some important questions about them. Unless you make at least this initial effort, until you engage in this primary level of examination and conscientiously ask yourself whether the actions you are doing are right or wrong or whether the things you are pursuing are good or bad, you have not taken even the first step toward an examined life.

Knowing What You Know

In Aeschylus's tragic drama *Agamemnon*, the victorious Greek king returns home after ten years at Troy, but he does not receive the welcome for which he was undoubtedly hoping. Soon after he steps off his chariot and enters the majestic hallway of his palace, strewn with flowers by his scheming wife Clytemnestra, she strikes. She catches him up in some robes, "as fishermen cast their huge circling nets," and with sword in hand thrusts three times.

> Thus he went down, and the life struggled out of him;
> and as he died he spattered me with the dark red
> and violent driven rain of bitter savored blood.[14]

Clytemnestra acts in bitter memory of the murder of their daughter, Iphigenia, whom Agamemnon had sacrificed on the altar at Aulis many years earlier in order to appease the gods and allow for the launching of the invasion of Troy. Now the mother will have her revenge. Having taken the innocent life of their beloved child, Agamemnon will pay with his own.

Although Clytemnestra is driven by intense feeling, she is not blinded by passion. There is no *akrasia* here. She knows exactly what she is doing, and she is doing it willingly and with no regret. She has had ten years to nurse her grievance, to mull over her anger, and plan the king's punishment upon his return. She exclaims,

> thus to me
> the conflict born of ancient bitterness is not
> a thing new thought upon, but pondered deep in time.[15]

Clytemnestra cannot be accused of not thinking before acting. She does not proceed toward so terrible a deed mindlessly. On the contrary, she has reflected long and hard on it. And she has done so, she claims, in the light of what she believes to be right. She is moved not only by anger but by principle. Her mind is on justice (*diké*), and in light of this principle she decides that the slayer must be slain. She insists that she has reason on her side and so is justified on moral grounds.

> With the sword he struck,
> with the sword he pays for his own act . . .
> Now hear you this, the right behind my sacrament.
> By my child's justice driven to fulfillment.[16]

Clytemnestra is certain of the righteousness of her action. She has a conception of justice as reciprocity and has chosen her deed on this basis.

An examined life? Hardly. While Clytemnestra, despite being moved by intense passion, may, in some sense, have engaged in the kind of reflection upon her action that constitutes the elementary level of examination, there is more to the examined life than just ensuring that your actions are an expression of your moral principles. At a more fundamental level, it is those moral beliefs themselves that must be examined. No longer may you simply take for granted the most important values that have served as guides in choosing goals and actions. They, too, must be subjected to critical inspection. You need to see whether your general beliefs about rightness and goodness are indeed justified, and thus whether you should continue to hold and use them. In this more advanced stage of the examined life, the very standards by which everything else is tested now get put to the test themselves.

Here lies Euthyphro's more serious failure. Even if he *can* explain why he thinks prosecuting his father is the pious thing to do, he really has no defensible idea about what piety is. Had he actually engaged in this higher level of examination, he would have been better prepared to respond to Socrates's questions and challenges. He should not feel too bad about being unable to explain the nature of piety, however, given the difficulty of the intellectual challenge, and Socrates would be the first to agree. Moreover, Euthyphro has a lot of company, some of it very distinguished. Plato's dialogues are full of characters who are tongue-tied when it comes to explaining basic moral matters, including those values that are essential to our well-being and, in some cases, at the heart of those characters' vocations. Charmides, a beautiful and charming young man, cannot say what temperance or self-control is; Lysis, in the company of his closest friends, admits his ignorance about the true character of friendship; and both Laches and Nicias, accomplished generals, are stuck when it comes to a fitting definition of courage. Even Socrates admits—perhaps sincerely, perhaps not—that he cannot define any of the virtues. Euthyphro's failure to successfully defend his beliefs about piety, then, is not all that remarkable.

Euthyphro's true flaw, and what he *should* feel ashamed about, is that he never even engaged in the kind of philosophical reflection that would have led him to recognize his own ignorance, whether about piety or any other morally significant topic on which he may have regarded himself an expert. It is one thing not to know; it an entirely another thing not to try to know.

Self-Examination

We have seen that when Socrates says to Euthyphro, "I hope you know what you are doing," he is asking him whether anything more than just a feeling or hunch about piety is guiding him in his choice of action. He wants assurance that Euthyphro is not acting blindly, without any firm beliefs whatsoever, but that the beliefs that *are* guiding his action are the correct ones, or at least ones that he can defend. The person leading the full life of examination does not just *think* that what he is doing is good—he *knows* it. And he knows it because his choice of action is informed by an *understanding* of what is good. Similarly, he knows that his actions are just or right because he understands justice or rightness.

The question, though, is, how does he acquire this understanding? What does the life of examination demand of a person when it comes to his beliefs on such matters, and especially the requisite testing of those beliefs? No one can say whether his action is just or right unless he knows the nature of justice or rightness. But how does he know *that* he knows what justice or rightness is? How does he ensure that he is acting on the basis of knowledge and not just random opinion, however true that opinion may happen to be?

One way of determining this is already familiar to anyone who has ever read one of Plato's dialogues or is even remotely familiar with "the Socratic method." Socrates's goal in all such conversations, as we saw in his exchange with Euthyphro, is to discover whether a person really does know what he or she claims to know. He pursues this through relentless questioning. First, ask the person to provide a definition of the concept ("What is piety?" "What is justice?"); then, challenge that definition to see if it withstands scrutiny. If it does not, refine the definition, or substitute an entirely new one, and try again. And do not give up until you arrive at a definition that can survive intense interrogation.

Before the testing can begin, however, there needs to be some clarity on the definition itself. What exactly does

Euthyphro mean when he says piety is what the gods love? It takes him several tries just to come up with a clear, workable definition. In Plato's *Republic*, a political dialogue focused on the nature and benefits of justice, when the character Thrasymachus insists that justice is simply whatever is advantageous to the powerful, Socrates first wants to know the meaning of such a claim.

Once a proposed definition of the principle or value in question has been settled upon and clarified, it is then subjected to examination. As we have seen, Socrates likes the method of *reductio ad absurdum*. Does the definition, taken in conjunction with other beliefs and principles—typically ones that are nonnegotiable or that enjoy universal agreement—lead ultimately to some kind of incoherence or contradiction? If so, then the definition must be jettisoned. This strategy, we saw, moved Socrates to reject Euthyphro's definition of piety. Pious actions cannot, by definition, be those that are loved by the gods, because actions that are loved by some gods are hated by others; and so by Euthyphro's definition, an action would be both pious and impious.

Alternatively, you might show that a proposed definition is directly inconsistent with some other, more fundamental beliefs that the person holds. A religious person who believes in God and who also believes that God is essentially just and good—and presumably these would be among this person's deepest convictions—cannot then claim that the nature of justice is determined solely by God's commandments or preferences. To say that some action is just only because God has commanded it renders trivial the claim that God itself is just. If justice is determined by God's commandment, then there is no independent, objective standard of justice by reference to which we can meaningfully assess God's own justice. A God who condones rape or torture, in this view, would thereby make rape and torture just actions. Similarly, if someone believes that morality is equivalent to what is legal and that justice is simply a matter of following the law, then in principle he cannot also believe that a law issued by the state can be unjust. If justice is determined by the law, then the notion of an unjust law would be incoherent. Thus, if this person is deeply committed to the idea that it is legitimate to protest a law that he deems unjust, perhaps a law that permits discrimination on the basis of skin color, then he must reject the definition of justice that makes it a function of civil legislation.

Another tried and true philosophical way of testing a belief is through the use of counter-examples. To show that someone's belief is unjustified, and perhaps even false, you might simply point to an example of something that is an exception or contrary to the belief. You can easily undermine the belief that all birds fly by showing that there are certain flightless birds (penguins and ostriches). Likewise, you might challenge someone's definition of justice by presenting either an instance of an act that he himself admits is just but that does not fit the definition or, alternatively, an instance of an act that seems clearly *unjust* but that satisfies the definition. As we have seen, it is irrational to persist in a belief that has been falsified; but it is also irrational to maintain as "knowledge" an opinion that faces an objection to which you are unable to respond successfully.

The Cartesian Method

Socrates thrived on the give-and-take of philosophical conversation. He would have been lost, unable to carry out his "divine mission," had there been no one willing to engage him in his characteristic activity of *elenchus*, or testing others through a persistent process of question and answer. (He uses this as a reason not to take the legally permissible option of making a counter-offer to the jury's death sentence with the less extreme penalty of exile from Athens, and even to refuse his friends' offer to help him escape from jail; no other city would allow him to philosophize as a social practice, so what would be the point of exile or escape?)[17] However, the testing of beliefs and values in an examined life does not require an actual dialogue. It can all be done quietly, as a first-person exercise. This is, in fact, how Descartes proceeds in the epistemological parts of the *Meditations on First Philosophy*.

The *Meditations* have long been regarded as an attempt by Descartes to refute skepticism, or the view that the absolute certainty required for true knowledge is not possible. Skeptics argue that, given the limitations of our faculties in a world constantly in flux, the best we can hope for in science and even ordinary life are relative probabilities.[18] Skepticism first flourished as a philosophical school in Hellenistic antiquity but enjoyed a revival in the sixteenth century with the rediscovery of ancient texts that presented the various arguments that skeptics used to undermine confidence in both ordinary and extraordinary knowledge claims. Michel de Montaigne (1533–92), for one, in the longest of his *Essays*, the "Apology for Raymond Sebond," rehearses the various "modes" of ancient skepticism for the purpose of dulling the allure of dogmatism and encouraging self-examination and humility in human affairs.[19] The inconsistency of our sense impressions of the external world (for example, when something looks bent from one perspective but straight from another), the disagreements in matters of reason (where what is true or right for one society or historical epoch is false or wrong for another), even the differences among cultures in what is to count as "rational"—all of this is taken by Montaigne and other skeptics as evidence that our faculties for knowing are unreliable. Our senses and reason give us, at best, opinion, not knowledge, and so it would be wise for us to adopt a properly humble epistemic attitude: Don't be so sure that you know what you think you know.

By the early seventeenth century, the "Pyrrhonian" revival of skepticism—so-called after the ancient skeptic Pyrrho of Ellis—is reported to have made inroads among certain European intellectual circles, including one frequented by Descartes. His seventeenth-century biographer Adrien Baillet tells a story of Descartes attending a gathering in Paris of "learned and inquisitive persons" at the home of the papal nuncio to hear a lecture by a scientist named Nicolas de Villiers, Lord of Chandoux. Baillet reports that Chandoux, no less than other modern thinkers, "sought to escape from the yoke of [medieval] Scholasticism" and argued in behalf of a "new philosophy . . . established on unassailable foundations." His presentation was roundly applauded by the assembled company, who approved of his refutation of the sterile and uninformative "[Aristotelian] philosophy ordinarily taught in the Schools." The lone holdout in the audience was Descartes. When one of Descartes's friends noticed his reticence and asked him why he did not join the others in praising the lecturer, Descartes replied that while he appreciated Chandoux's attack on Scholastic philosophy, he was not pleased by his willingness, despite claiming to seek "unassailable foundations," to settle for mere probability in the quest for knowledge. "He [Descartes] added that when it was a matter of people easy-going enough to be satisfied with probabilities, as was the case with the illustrious company before which he had the honor to speak, it was not difficult to pass off the false for the true, and in turn to make the true pass for the false in favor of appearances. To prove this on the spot, he asked

for someone in the assembled group to take the trouble to propose whatever truth he wanted, one among those that appear
to be the most incontestable."

Someone stepped up to the challenge, Baillet says, where-
upon Descartes, "with a dozen arguments each more probable
than the other," proved to the assembled company that the
proposition they all thought true was false. Then, also with
probabilistic reasoning, Descartes turned around and demonstrated that a proposition that they were convinced was false is
true. He "then proposed a falsehood of the sort that is ordinarily taken to be most evidently false, and by means of another
dozen probable arguments, he brought his hearers to the point
of taking this falsehood for a plausible truth. The assembly was
surprised by the force and extent of the genius that M. Descartes exhibited in his reasoning but was even more astonished
to be so clearly convinced of how easily their minds could be
duped by probability."[20] When asked whether he knew of some
other, better means for avoiding error and arriving at truth, Descartes replied that he knew none more infallible than the one
he had himself been using, and that there did not seem to be
any truth that he could not clearly demonstrate with *certainty*
using the principles of his own method. The story is often taken
to show that, for Descartes, to settle for mere probability and
thus give up the search for absolute certainty is to concede too
much to the philosophical skeptic.

In the *Meditations*, however, Descartes does have a grander,
more important goal than simply refuting skepticism as an epistemological exercise. Aside from demonstrating the possibility
of knowledge in the face of the skeptical challenge, Descartes
intends to provide solid and indubitable foundations for
science—for *his* science, the new mechanistic physics of nature.[21] This means, first of all, a new approach to knowledge,

something to replace the old method of knowing that guided Aristotelian-Scholastic science. Second, Descartes believes that the employment of this new, modern way of knowing would lead to absolutely certain "first principles." These general epistemological and metaphysical foundations, once established, would in turn ground a theory of nature (physics in the broadest sense), which in turn would support the scientific explanations of natural phenomena that constitute more particular sciences, including biology, astronomy, and medicine.

The *Meditations*, in providing the foundations for natural science, is, above all, a book about mind, body, and God.[22] This is the real content of "first philosophy." Descartes wants to show what he, using reason and his own method of inquiry, can discover about the soul, material things, and their Creator, and how the most basic understanding of these general topics can lead to other, even more useful knowledge. Writing a few years after the publication of the work, Descartes employs the metaphor of a tree to explain how he sees the entire structure of human knowledge. "The whole of philosophy is like a tree. The roots are metaphysics, the trunk is physics, and the branches emerging from the trunk are all the other sciences, which may be reduced to three principal ones, namely medicine, mechanics, and morals."[23] In the *Meditations*, Descartes tends primarily to the roots of the tree of knowledge, which contain "the principles of knowledge, including the explanation of the principal attributes of God, the non-material nature of our souls and all the clear and distinct notions which are in us."[24] But none of these truths will be revealed to the "Meditator" (Descartes) as he narrates his cognitive itinerary until after he accomplishes a kind of intellectual cleansing and reorientation.

This is where "examination" comes in. Descartes tells the reader in the "Synopsis" that serves as a preface to the work that one of his goals is to "free us from all our preconceived opinions and provide the easiest route by which the mind may be led away from the senses."[25] He wants to empty the mind of prejudices, some left over from childhood, that may hinder proper inquiry into nature, and to redirect our attention from the confusing and misleading testimony of random sense experience toward the clear and distinct ideas of the intellect. If knowledge is to emerge from the jumble of beliefs in his mind, Descartes needs first to clear out garbage.

The starting point of this process is the so-called method of doubt. Progressing in a systematic manner, Descartes will consider all of his mind's contents, all of his beliefs and judgments, in order to see if there is something, anything, that is not merely ungrounded prejudice or the sort of haphazardly acquired opinion (whether true or false) that Socrates rued but rather real knowledge, an absolutely indubitable certainty. In effect, through the method of doubt, Descartes extends skepticism to its most radical position—not for the sake of undermining human knowledge but in order to beat the skeptic at his own game. If Descartes can show that there are certain epistemically unassailable beliefs even for someone who is in the midst of an extreme skeptical crisis, where everything is subjected to the possibility of doubt, then the reconstruction of the edifice of knowledge, especially scientific knowledge, can begin on that secure basis.

Descartes was fond of comparing this procedure to more familiar sorts of activities, such as tearing down a house and rebuilding it from the ground up because its foundation was unstable, or going through a barrel of apples to see if there are any that have gone bad and whose rot might spread to the good fruit. "Suppose [a person] had a basket full of apples and, being worried that some of the apples were rotten, wanted to take out the rotten ones to prevent the rot from spreading. How would he proceed? Would he not begin by tipping the whole lot out of the basket? And would not the next step be to cast his eye over each apple in turn, and pick up and put back in the basket only those he saw to be sound, leaving the others?" In the first stage of his project, Descartes will tip over the contents of his mind, "to separate the false beliefs from the others, so as to prevent their contaminating the rest and making the whole lot uncertain. Now the best way they can accomplish this is to reject all their beliefs together in one go, as if they were all uncertain and false. They can then go over each belief in turn and re-adopt only those which they recognize to be true and indubitable."[26] He knows that this is not an easy thing to do and that it requires an uncomfortable degree of critical self-examination. However, as Descartes says at the beginning of the *Meditations*, the task must be undertaken at least once in your life, if only to see what one does know and, more important, *can* know. "I realized that it was necessary, once in a lifetime, to demolish everything completely and start again right from the foundations if I wanted to establish anything at all in the sciences that was stable and likely to last."[27]

Descartes begins the exercise by noting that many things that people ordinarily and uncritically take to be certain can in fact be subjected to doubt. There are, for example, the simple (and easily resolvable) doubts that arise when one apprehends objects under less than ideal circumstances. For example, it is easy to mistake the size or shape of something when it is perceived at a distance or in poor light. The lesson here is that the senses are not *always* to be trusted, that not everything they report about the external world is true. "From time to time, I have found that the senses deceive, and it is prudent never to trust completely those who have deceived us even once." These kinds of errors, however, are not very serious, and you can guard against them through careful examination of what the senses are reporting and whether they are operating in conditions that favor their accuracy: Is the lighting good? Do you have your glasses on? Are you sober?

On the other hand, there are many other beliefs about the world that even the most careful and critical observer ordinarily accepts as certain. These constitute some of the core beliefs of common sense, such as that one has a body, that there is in fact an external world full of other bodies, and that things in that world are basically as they appear to be under the best observational conditions. "Although the senses occasionally deceive us with respect to objects which are very small or in the distance, there are many other beliefs about which doubt is quite impossible, even though they are derived from the senses—for example, that I am here, sitting by the fire, wearing a winter dressing-gown, holding this piece of paper in my hands, and so on." What could be more certain than that there is a world out there—independent from our minds—made up of familiar objects?

And yet, Descartes continues, even these apparently indubitable beliefs can be put into doubt. After all, one is often deceived by dreams, in which fantasies are mistaken for reality. "How often, asleep at night, am I convinced of just such familiar events—that I am here in my dressing-gown, sitting by the fire—when in fact I am lying undressed in bed!" Perhaps, the skeptical Descartes suggests, he is only *dreaming* that he is sitting by the fire, holding a piece of paper, or has a body, in which case it would all be an illusion and these most evident beliefs would in fact be false. The experiences of dream-life can be so realistic, so similar to experiences in waking life, that you cannot tell whether you are awake or dreaming; thus, on any given occasion, your experience of an independent reality may, in truth, not be such. Or, to put the doubt another way, even granting that you can know when you are awake and when you are asleep, the qualitative similarity—the experiential vividness, the composition of things, their shapes and colors, and so on— between dreams (which are known to be illusory) and waking life (which is assumed to be veridical) raises the question whether the appearances of waking life are not just as illusory as our dreams?[28] Dream experiences are not to be trusted, so why should any more credence be given to waking experiences, since, as far as experience can tell, the two seem indistinguishable? Thus, the level of doubt deepens—and his confidence in the senses as a source of knowledge about the world diminishes—as Descartes continues his quest for something certain.

And yet, even if all sensory experiences are no more veridical than dreams, must there not at least be a world out there, an external realm of things that, if not exactly resembling what is presented by the senses, is at least *somewhat* like the contents of ordinary experience? Where would the stuff of dreams come from if there were not *something* outside me that is their ultimate causal source? "It surely must be admitted that the visions which come in sleep are like paintings, which must have been fashioned in the likeness of things that are real, and hence that at least these general kinds of things—eyes, head, hands, and the body as a whole—are things which are not imaginary but are real and exist. For even when painters try to create sirens and satyrs with the most extraordinary bodies, they cannot give them natures which are new in all respects; they simply jumble up the limbs of different animals."[29]

Or maybe, Descartes continues, there are not even such "general kinds of things" in an external world, and maybe no external world at all. Still, surely there can be no doubting the reality of "even simpler and more general things," such as the "eternal truths" of mathematics. These are perhaps the most basic and indubitable items imaginable. Moreover, they do not require the existence "in nature" of anything, since they seem to be only simple, abstract, but objectively true concepts discovered by the understanding. So, Descartes says, let it be granted that all those sciences that depend on the actual existence of things in nature are now uncertain—"that physics, astronomy, medicine, and all other disciplines which depend on the study of composite things are doubtful." Nonetheless, he suggests, arithmetic, geometry, and other purely rational disciplines that require only such items as number and the concept of three-dimensional extension, "which deal only with the simplest and most general things, regardless of whether they really exist in nature or not," would appear to remain true and certain. "For whether I am awake or asleep," Descartes says, "two and three added together are five."[30]

However, if the epistemological challenge of the First Meditation is to be consistently pursued to the end, even these apparently most certain truths have to be put to the test in order to see if there is any conceivable reason for doubting them. Are the principles of mathematics in fact real and objective truths, as they seem to be, or simply compelling fictions concocted by the mind? This is where Descartes takes the exercise, as if it has not gone far enough, to what he calls a "hyperbolic" level. For he now entertains the radical possibility that, while he *may* have been created by an omnipotent God—and this is not yet certain either, but appears to be only "a long-standing opinion"—he presently has no persuasive reason to believe that this creator is not a deceiver who allows him regularly to go astray even in those cases where he thinks he has "the most perfect knowledge." How, Descartes asks, can he be sure that he does not go wrong "every time I add two and three or count the sides of a square, or in some even simpler matter, if that is imaginable?" For all Descartes knows at this point, God, or whoever his creator may be, loves to see him in error and thus has intentionally given him a faulty and unreliable mind—a mental faculty that, even when used properly and carefully, produces nothing but false beliefs. Descartes may feel compelled to believe that two plus three equals five, because his intellect tells him so; but maybe, just because his intellect has its origin in an all-powerful and deceptive deity and therefore is systematically unreliable, that proposition is not in fact true.

Descartes suggests that this kind of doubt is even more cogent if "the author of my being" is not God but simply the random forces of nature. Let us assume, then, "that I have arrived at my present state by fate or chance or a continuous chain of events, or by some other means; yet since deception and error seem to be imperfections, the less powerful they make my original cause, the more likely it is that I am so imperfect as to be deceived all the time."[31] Whether Descartes was created by a God of unknown, and possibly vicious, character, or his existence is the result of happenstance, is immaterial. Either scenario raises serious doubts about the reliability of his faculties, including reason itself. For all Descartes knows, he is deceived even with respect to those things that seem to him to be the most certain. Maybe because of his inherently defective nature nothing at all that Descartes *thinks* to be true, no matter how subjectively certain he may feel about it, really *is* true. "I am finally compelled to admit that there is not one of my former beliefs about which a doubt may not properly be raised."

Descartes's descent into a deep skeptical crisis is, by the end of the First Meditation, complete. Some of the doubts are generated by highly improbable and fantastic considerations. At one point, in order to reinforce the uncertainty engendered by the case of dreams—the force of habit is strong, he says, and it is hard "not to slide back into my old opinions"—he even considers the possibility (reminiscent of the "Evil Enchanter" that Don Quixote believes is tormenting him)[32] that all of his sensory experiences are merely "phantasms" and illusions generated not by God but by an all-powerful evil deceiver, a "malicious demon" intent on deceiving him. Descartes insists that such considerations, however unlikely, are to be taken seriously in this philosophical moment if he is to discover something that is absolutely certain and immune to any doubt whatsoever. For the purpose of reestablishing the edifice of knowledge on secure foundations, every possibility of doubt must be allowed. While there may certainly be, among the things that Descartes had believed, many that really *are* true, he needs to come up with some reliable way to distinguish these from what is false or doubtful.

Perhaps Descartes has carried examination too far. By the end of the First Meditation there seems to be nothing left: truths have disappeared, but also the means of acquiring truths. How can Descartes, having played the skeptic all too well, now hope, as he does, to reasonably prove God's existence and benevolence and, thus, the reliability of his God-given reason? How can he rely on reason to validate his rationality without arguing in a circle? His cognitive cleansing may have been so radical that, by thoroughly undermining his sensory and rational faculties, there is now no hope of ever gaining knowledge. Descartes's contemporary critics, in fact, accused him of actually *being* a skeptic and an atheist who, under the ruse of trying to find knowledge, hoped ultimately to show that knowledge, including knowledge of God, is not possible.

The Essential Questions

Descartes's extraordinary, radical, and highly imaginative strategy, while of great historical importance, is certainly not for everyone; indeed, perhaps it makes sense only in its seventeenth-century European context. Nonetheless, his enterprise in the *Meditations*—which he is certain will not just lay the foundations for his scientific project but also have practical implications for how he is to live—is an example of examination at its finest. Descartes, like Socrates, is urging that at least once in your life (*semel in vita*, he says in Latin) you need to stop and ask yourself some very difficult questions.

These need to be, first of all, questions about what you are doing. But more important, they need to be epistemological questions about the beliefs you appeal to when you decide what to do. You need to examine your actions *and* the values, ideals, and principles that guide them. You need to see whether you really do know what you think you know. To satisfy fully the demands of the examined life requires that you give some thought to what you believe—whether those beliefs are moral beliefs, as we have been concentrating on, or political beliefs, or religious beliefs, or aesthetic beliefs—and determine whether those beliefs are epistemically justified.

Do you believe that vaccinations cause autism? Ask yourself: *Why* do I believe this? Do I really have good and compelling evidence—evidence that meets the standards of medical science—to support this claim?

Do you believe that the campaign against climate change is based on a hoax perpetrated by liberal scientists? Again, ask yourself: *Why* do I believe this? Who or what is the source of my information? Is this source scientifically sound and unbiased, or does it simply feed some political, religious, or social prejudices?

Does your belief that 5G networks are linked to the spread of COVID-19 rest on a careful examination of the properties of 5G transmissions, a mastery of how the human immune system operates, and a thorough understanding of the coronavirus (which, to this day, scientists deny possessing)?

This question about *why* we believe something may be the most important question of all, and is likely the key to curing bad thinking. Sadly, it is a question all-to-rarely asked.

Socratic (Human) Wisdom

Earlier we looked at some traditional, pre-Socratic conceptions of wisdom. We closed with the suggestion that Socrates brought about a philosophical transformation of that all-important virtue, turning its gaze inward. No longer grounded in study of the world around us, wisdom for Socrates became the study of oneself. The wise person can give an account, a *logos*, not of natural phenomena but of her own manner of thinking and living.

The oracle at Delphi, when consulted by Socrates's friend Chairephon, famously declared that "no one is wiser than Socrates."[33] Socrates, for his part, claims to be puzzled by this divine pronouncement, since he considers himself *not* wise. "When I heard of this reply [of the oracle] I asked myself: 'Whatever does the god mean? What is his riddle? I am very conscious that I am not wise at all; what then does he mean by saying that I am the wisest? For surely he does not lie; it is not legitimate for him to do so.'"[34] He allows that there is a kind of wisdom that others possess—just the kind of wisdom that we have seen consists in the knowledge that informs a skill or

techné. Craftsmen, politicians, even poets all have a highly specialized *sophia* that endows them with a narrowly confined expertise. However, their wisdom ends where their craft ends.
Unfortunately, Socrates realizes, these individuals, proud of
their limited wisdom, also believe themselves to know things
that in fact they do not know. "Each of them, because of his
success at his craft, thought himself very wise in other, most
important pursuits." This is what Socrates discovered as he went
around questioning people. The poet, for example, knows how
to make fine poetry about gods and heroes, but he then thinks,
quite wrongly, that he really knows something about divinities,
politics, and war—that is, about piety, justice, and courage. His
epistemic arrogance offsets his craft-knowledge. "He thought
himself wise," Socrates says, "but he was not."[35]

Now, Socrates does not claim to have any real craft-
knowledge. He has no special skills by which to distinguish
himself or even just make a living (he was a stonecutter by
trade, but none too successful). In this sense, his denial of wisdom can be taken at face value. Nor does he pretend to have
that knowledge of "most important pursuits . . . a wisdom more
than human" that others clearly lack. It may be that he does not
tell Euthyphro what piety is, or Laches what courage is, or
Meno how virtue is acquired, because he himself really does *not*
know such things; this is a question long debated by scholars.[36]
Be that as it may, this kind of supreme wisdom, Socrates suggests, is primarily for the gods.

Is the oracle wrong, then? No, of course not. Oracles are
never wrong. They just need to be interpreted properly. And
this is precisely what Socrates does. "What has caused my reputation is none other than a certain kind of wisdom. What kind
of wisdom? Human wisdom, perhaps. . . . I am wiser than
[some other man]; it is likely that neither of us knows anything

worthwhile, but he thinks he knows something when he does not, whereas when I do not know, neither do I think I know; so I am likely to be wiser than [others] to this small extent, that I do not think I know what I do not know."[37] Here, then, is the meaning of the oracle's pronouncement and the true nature of wisdom: No one is wiser than Socrates because he alone knows that he knows nothing.

It is important to note that wisdom, in this sense, does not require knowing nothing. Socrates professes a lack of knowledge, but that is not what is essential here. Wisdom is not ignorance per se. Nor is it even a skepticism about the possibility of knowledge. Being wise does not mean that you forfeit any legitimate claim to a substantive body of knowledge. Socrates's wisdom does not consist in his not knowing anything. Nor does it consist in the trivial fact that he, at least, knows *one* thing that no one else seems to know, namely, that he knows nothing.[38] Rather, what matters—and this constitutes Socrates's real contribution to the development of the notion of wisdom—is that, as he says, "when I do not know, neither do I think I know."

In other words, wisdom is intimately connected with the life of examination. It is just that kind of reflection on your beliefs and values at the heart of an examined life that allows you to determine what exactly you *do* know—or, at least, what you are truly justified in believing. This is not a purely intellectual exercise, however, since, as we have seen, without examination there is no hope of acting well.

As for "bad thinking," it should be clear by now that the alternative, "good thinking," just *is* the life of examination, the philosophical life. The cure for bad thinking—and, ultimately, bad action—is Socratic wisdom. This entails learning how to examine—how to analyze and assess—not just what others are saying, but what you believe, and especially what you ought and ought not to believe. It means avoiding precipitous convictions and only giving your assent to what is accompanied by reliable evidence; abandoning beliefs for which there is no evidence, or even counter-evidence; and developing the practice of good, logically sound reasoning and knowing how to put that reasoning to work in your practical and moral life.

All of this is precisely the subject matter of philosophy. Unfortunately, we seem—as individuals and as a society—to be less engaged than ever with these important epistemic practices. We can only hope that it is not too late to reverse this trend toward an apparent species-wide epidemic of bad thinking. In the end, philosophy and the examined life may be our best, and perhaps only, prospect to save us, and our planet, from ourselves.

Conclusion

Thinking Responsibly

Bad thinking is like a virus. It spreads. It infects all strata of society, in domains both private and public. It is there lurking in the home, at work, in business and government. It attacks parents, children, politicians, shopkeepers, lawyers, doctors, movie stars, teachers—all of us. It is potent and it is dangerous. Bad thinking harms the mind: it generates unfounded beliefs and leads us astray in our opinions. And because our beliefs are so closely tied to our emotions, it corrupts our affective lives as well: our love, our hate, our envy and jealousy, and especially our hopes and fears can all be distorted by bad thinking.

Bad thinking harms our material lives as well. As it brings about failures of judgment, it leads to thoughtless behavior and immoral actions. In the public sphere it generates uninformed, misguided, and destructive policies that undermine our health and well-being and poison our environment.

There is, however, an antidote for bad thinking, a way to mitigate its effects and even prevent it altogether. It lies in the right kind of education, a kind of "emendation of the intellect" (to use Spinoza's phrase) through philosophy and, more generally, the humanities. Philosophy, as we have shown, teaches the canons of good thinking, that is, proper reasoning and the epistemic, moral, and even political benefits of forming and holding beliefs in a rational manner. As Socrates insisted, a philosophical life—a life of self-examination in what one believes and values and what one does—is a good and worthwhile life, and its rewards are precious.

Of course, training in critical reasoning, conscientious deliberation, and considerate judgment is not the purview of philosophy alone. The disciplines that make up the core of the humanities—history (including the history of science and of art); literature; cultural, ethnic, and linguistic studies—all contribute to the kind of reflective and critical awareness of self, of others, and of the world that is essential to alleviating the pandemic of careless, narrow, and irrational thinking that currently threatens us as individuals, as citizens of our respective nations, and as inhabitants of the only planet that will have us. Those who dismiss the theory of evolution through natural selection as "just a theory" need robust lessons in the history and methodology of science, and the novels of Jane Austen are populated with illuminating examples of bad thinking and the perils of an unexamined life.

Of course, philosophy and other humanities alone cannot save us. People are not going to give up cherished and long-held beliefs just because you point out to them that those beliefs are irrational, even false, or that they did not come to those beliefs in a philosophically responsible way. No matter how educated or cultivated we are—no matter how much philosophy, science, history, literature, and art we are familiar with—there will always be reasons why we stand by beliefs and practices that, from a rational standpoint, should be abandoned. Epistemic and normative stubbornness is not so easily overcome. There are often very personal, nonrational reasons why we believe, and will continue to believe, the things we do and resist giving those beliefs up. Emotion and desire are strong barriers to examination and the revision of opinion. The belief in God, for example, brings consolation to a great many people of faith. At the same time, it often prevents people from accepting rationally justified beliefs when they conflict with dogma. Ideology, too, can keep us from seeing the error of our cognitive ways. When certain opinions mesh well with our political persuasions, we are more likely to accept them and to persist in them, despite evidence that they are false. Socratic self-examination is a discomforting, and disorienting, experience.

Even the best-educated people will have extended bouts of epistemic and normative stubbornness. In a 2019 book, *Why Trust Science?*, the science historian Naomi Oreskes points out that "if we define success in terms of cultural authority, the success of science is clearly not only incomplete but at the moment looking rather shaky. Large numbers of our fellow citizens—including the current president and vice president of the United States—doubt and in some cases actively challenge scientific conclusions about vaccines, evolution, climate change, and even the harms of tobacco. These challenges cannot be dismissed as 'scientific illiteracy.'" The problem is not a lack of knowledge or education, but, in many cases, political allegiance. Oreskes notes, for example, that "the more educated Republicans are, the more likely they are to doubt or reject scientific claims about anthropogenic climate change. This indicates not a lack of knowledge but the effects of ideological motivation, interpreted self-interest, and the power of competing beliefs."[1] She recognizes the difficulty in overcoming such impediments to a more reasonable life but suggests that an important first step is "exposing the ideological and economic motivations underlying science denial, to demonstrate that the objections are not scientific, but political."[2]

Moreover, as the philosopher Heather Douglas has shown, a person's assessment of evidence—what does and does not count in favor of a belief—is often grounded not in epistemic factors but moral, ethical, political, and economic ones. Thus, some will discount the scientific evidence in favor of the human causes of climate change when political or economic interests are at stake.[3] They will simply write off any evidence that disconfirms their beliefs as "fake news," and contrary narratives as lies.

(Then there are those who, for career advancement, money, power, and/or influence encourage false beliefs in others—for example, by dismissing scientific consensus on the COVID-19 pandemic as a "hoax" or by sowing doubt about clear and unassailable facts, such as the birthplace of President Barack Obama or the security of mail-in ballots. A number of well-known television pundits come to mind. But that is an entirely different story, one of mendacity rather than stubbornness.)

What, then, accounts for epistemic stubbornness? Why do we refuse to engage in the kind of rational accountability that would save us from ourselves? Is it emotion? ideology? efficiency? laziness? insecurity? Has natural selection shaped us in ways that make poor reasoning as irresistible as the sweet and fatty foods responsible for escalating rates of diabetes, obesity, and other afflictions? These are questions for psychologists to answer. What is clear is that unless we can turn things around and become epistemically more responsible in our beliefs and, more generally, commit ourselves to living examined lives, the health of our minds, of our bodies, of our democracies, and of our planet are in grave danger.

Notes

Introduction: Our Epistemological Crisis

1. Krugman 2020.
2. See Nadler 2017.
3. Plumer and Davenport 2019.

Chapter 1: Thinking, Bad and Good

1. Clifford 1877, 294.
2. Clifford 1877, 294.
3. Descartes 1984, 2:41.
4. Descartes 1984, 2:40–41.
5. Clifford 1877, 295.
6. Clifford 1877, 289.
7. Clifford 1877, 289.
8. Clifford 1877, 290.
9. Clifford 1877, 295.
10. Pascal 1966, 149–50.
11. James 1956.
12. Hviid et al. 2019.
13. Pollock 1986.
14. However, the idea that having a true justified belief is sufficient for knowledge was critiqued by the philosopher Edmund Gettier in a famous 1963 article (Gettier 1963). The subsequent debate in epistemology has been intense.

Chapter 2: How to Be Reasonable

1. Doyle 2016b, 17.
2. Doyle 2016a, 17.

3. However, not all deductive arguments are formally valid. For example, consider the argument: All the objects in the drawer are shirts, therefore all the objects in the drawer are clothes. This is valid because if the premise is true, the conclusion must also be true. But the argument is not formally valid, because it does not always follow from a premise of the form "All Xs are Y" that "All Xs are Z." For instance, it does not follow from the fact that all the animals in the cage are gerbils that all the animals in the cage are snakes. In the following we will ignore these subtleties and treat validity as a purely formal notion.

4. If you do not know what an island is, then this might be valuable as an explanation of the meaning of "island." However, if intended as a means of convincing you that Madagascar is an island, the argument is a failure.

Chapter 3: Thinking and Explaining

1. Wainer and Zwerling 2006.

2. This is the conclusion drawn in Wainer and Zwerling 2006.

3. Kahneman 2011, 117–18.

4. This case is discussed in Wainer and Zwerling 2006.

5. Bacon 1939, 36, *The New Organon*, bk. 1, aphorism 46.

6. Wason 1960.

7. Wason 1966; Wason 1968.

8. Interestingly, although this experiment is a classic in the study of confirmation bias, and confirmation bias is typically construed as an unwarranted preference for observations that confirm a favorite hypothesis, in the sense of providing inductive support for the hypothesis, the correct solution to the card task actually involves deductive reasoning.

9. As the task with the cards reveals, this is true as well in the context of deductive reasoning.

10. Popper 1959.

11. For a history of the antivaccination movement, see Cummins 2019.

12. For a study involving over 650,000 children and also for references to other studies, see Hviid et al. 2019.

13. Perrigo 2020.

14. For a useful survey of the psychological literature on confirmation bias, as well as many illuminating examples of its pervasiveness, see Nickerson 1998.

15. Tversky and Kahneman 1982.

16. Gigerenzer and Hoffrage 1995.

17. The caution about base rates applies as well to what we have been calling enumerative induction, as is clear in the case involving the cabs, where the hypothesis

about which cab was involved in the accident draws on evidence involving the frequency of blue and green cabs.

18. See the interview with James Fetzer in Crawford 2020.

19. Appiah 2020.

Chapter 4: When Bad Thinking Becomes Bad Behavior

1. Berlin 2013.

2. Plato, *Statesman* 266e.

3. Aristotle, *Politics* 1253a.

4. Vigdor 2019.

5. Stack 2019.

6. The actor Tom Hanks, as famous a celebrity as there is, recalls being unable to buy a beer at a music festival because he did not have the wristband that the festival gave only to attendees who were over twenty-one; Hanks was sixty-two at the time. Hanks was interviewed on the Graham Norton Show, series 25, episode 12, June 21, 2019, https://www.bbc.co.uk/programmes/p07dpvx7/player.

7. Hart 1961, 21.

8. See, for example, Berlin 2002; Larmore 1987; Williams 1981.

9. For an elegant and extended discussion of moral conflict in ancient philosophy and literature, see Nussbaum 2001.

10. See, for example, Thomas Nagel's essay "War and Massacre" (Nagel 1991, 53–74).

11. The Madison disciplinarians could have benefited, as well, from acknowledging another philosophical concept, about language: the use/mention distinction. When you say, "You are an idiot," you are using the term 'idiot' to insult someone. When you say, "I am using the term 'idiot' to insult you," or "The word 'idiot' has five letters," or "Do not call me by the word 'idiot,'" you are only mentioning or referring to the term, not using it. But that is another story.

12. See Aristotle, *Nicomachean Ethics* 1106a26–b7. All translations from this work come from Aristotle 1985b.

13. For this reason, "rule utilitarians"—who argue that you should choose the action that, as a rule, tends to increase happiness, even when the performance of the action in the present circumstances does not actually increase happiness—insist that they have at least a practical advantage over "act utilitarians," who insist that the proper guide is the overall utility of the particular performance of the action in the present circumstances.

14. This is certainly not to say that the blind rule follower gives up responsibility for his action. After all, one is responsible for one's choice of rule in the first place, as well as the decision to apply the rule to the extent that one does.

15. Notice that this is not, strictly speaking, a legal matter. The law says only that you may not sell alcoholic beverages to minors; it does not say that you may not sell alcohol except to someone who produces proper identification. It is the business owner who has established that latter regulation, and thus it is perfectly within the rights of the business to allow employees to sell alcohol to people who are, obviously and without question, well above the minimum age. So in this case, the ultimate responsibility for judgment may lie with the owner or manager of the business.

16. Ovid, *Metamorphoses* 7.17–21; the translation is from Ovid 2004, 249.

17. Plato, *Phaedrus* 237e–238a, 246a–254e; the translation is from Plato 1961. The Greek term that the translator renders as "wantonness" is *hubris*.

18. Spinoza, *Ethics*, pt. 4, prop. 15; the translation is from Spinoza 1985.

19. Aristotle, *De motu animalium* 701a20; the translation is from Aristotle 1985a.

20. Aristotle, *Nicomachean Ethics* 1140a25–30, 1140b5.

21. Strictly speaking, the conclusion of a practical syllogism is not a proposition about what to do but the action itself.

22. Aristotle, *Nicomachean Ethics* 1140a10.

23. Aristotle, *Nicomachean Ethics* 1144a25.

24. The literature on Aristotle on *akrasia* is voluminous. For starters, there is Broadie 1991, chap. 5; Gottlieb 2009, chap. 8.5; Hutchinson 1995, 215–17; Mele 1999; Wiggins 1980.

25. Aristotle, *Nicomachean Ethics* 1147b30–32 and 1147b25.

26. Aristotle, *Nicomachean Ethics* 1150b20.

27. Aristotle, *Nicomachean Ethics* 1152a14–15.

28. Aristotle, *Nicomachean Ethics* 1147b15.

29. See, for example, Kraut 2018.

30. Plato, *Protagoras* 357d–e; the translation is from Plato 1961.

31. Railton 1986.

32. Hume 1978, 579–86.

33. Nagel 1970; Scanlon 1998; Shafer-Landau 2003.

34. Shafer-Landau 2003, 129–30; Svavarsdóttir 1999. Strictly speaking, internalists claim that moral beliefs necessarily motivate by themselves, so some philosophers— those who agree that moral beliefs can motivate on their own but do not necessarily do so—reject internalism.

35. Recent research in psychology seems to support the externalist position, that, beyond reasoning, the emotions play an essential role in motivating (or failing to motivate) moral behavior; see, for example, Aronson, Wilson and Akert 2019,

especially chapters 7–9. Haidt (2001 and 2012) has argued that moral "reasoning" is, in fact, less a matter of reasoning or rational deliberation than it is an intuitive judgment driven by emotion.

36. Of course, beyond the somewhat simplistic classical accounts of *akrasia* (where emotion or passion overpowers reason), there may be many other factors—having to do with self-control, social pressures (e.g., a desire to belong), impulsive behavior, psychopathy and addiction—that can explain why we fail to act in accordance with our best moral judgments. Moreover, neuroscientists have shown that morality has a neurobiological basis in the human brain; see, for example, Mendez 2006. Damasio and colleagues have studied the ways in which damage to the brain can impair moral behavior by interfering with affective response; see Anderson et al. 1999; Bechara et al. 1994; and Damasio 1994 and 1996. Our thanks to Patricia Churchland for pointing us to this dimension of the problem. Because we are interested in the issue primarily as a philosophical topic, however, we do not address the scientific literature.

37. Aristotle, *Nicomachean Ethics* 1148a15 and 1150b30.

38. Aristotle thus distinguishes between acting in ignorance and acting from or because of ignorance, and argues that we are responsible for actions only in the latter case. A person who is drunk will be acting in ignorance of what he is doing, but this does not make his action involuntary; see, for example, *Nicomachean Ethics* 1110a.

Chapter 5: Wisdom

1. When we discuss in this book what "Socrates" believed or said, we are referring not to the historical Socrates—from whom we have no writings—but to the character presented in most of Plato's dialogues. This fictional Socrates was modeled on the historical figure, whom Plato, Socrates's student, knew well. For an overview of the "Socrates problem," that is, distinguishing the historical Socrates from the literary "Socrates," see Dorion 2011.

2. Recently, however, this has changed for the better. For contemporary philosophical approaches to wisdom, see Kekes 1983; the essays in Lehrer et al. 1996; Nozick 1989; and Tiberius 2008. For a good overview, see Ryan 2018. The "big" philosophical question of the "meaning of life" is also enjoying renewed attention among philosophers; see, for example, the essays in Benatar 2010; Cottingham 2003; Kraut 2007; and Wolf 2010.

3. Nozick 1989, 269.

4. Kekes 1983, 277.

5. The episode appears in Herodotus, *The Histories* 3.82; all translations are from Herodotus 1954.

6. Homer, *Iliad* 5.50–54; translations are from Homer 1951.

7. Aristotle, *Nicomachean Ethics*, 1141a.

8. Homer, *Iliad* 1.250–52.

9. See Plato, *Protagoras* 343a.

10. The story of the encounter between Croesus and Solon is in Herodotus, *The Histories* 1.29–45.

11. Diels and Kranz 1974, 21; Barnes 1982, 11.

12. Diels and Kranz 1974, 22; Barnes 1982, 40.

13. Plato, *Phaedo* 96a–b (translation from Plato 1961).

14. Sellars 1962, 35.

15. Diels and Kranz 1974, 22; Barnes 1982, 1.

16. For illuminating recent studies of the beginnings of philosophy in ancient Greece, see Hadot 2004 and Sassi 2018. On wisdom in ancient philosophy, see Cooper 2012.

17. Diels and Kranz 1974, 21; Barnes 1982, 34.

18. Diels and Kranz 1974, 22; Barnes 1982, 41.

19. Xenophon, *Memorabilia* 1.1; all translations are from Xenophon 1979.

20. Xenophon, *Memorabilia* 1.1.

21. Nozick 1989, 267, 269.

Chapter 6: The Examined Life

1. For an illuminating discussion of Socrates's conception of the examined life, see Kraut 2006.

2. Plato, *Euthyphro* 9d; all translations are from Plato 1981.

3. Plato, *Euthyphro* 15c–e.

4. Plato, *Euthyphro* 4e.

5. A character from ancient Greek mythology. This sea-god was notoriously difficult to capture because of his ability constantly to change shape.

6. Plato, *Euthyphro* 15c–e; italics are ours.

7. There is a good deal of scholarly debate as to whether Socrates does indeed accept this principle, often called the "Socratic fallacy"; see, for example, Benson 2000 and 2013; Futter 2019; and Geach 1966.

8. 'Apology [Apologia]' in this context has its more uncommon meaning, a "defense." Socrates was absolutely not apologizing for his actions in the more typical sense of the word, as in expressing regret.

9. Plato, *Apology of Socrates* 29d–e; all translations are from Plato 1981.

10. Plato, *Apology of Socrates* 37e–38a.

11. Hume 1978, 2.3.3.

12. Plato, *Apology of Socrates* 28b.

13. Plato, *Apology of Socrates* 39c–d (italics are ours). In this passage, Socrates does not actually use the word *logos* for "an account" but rather *elenchon*, which is a noun corresponding to the method of examination that Socrates uses on his interlocutors, *elenchus*. To give an *elenchon* is, nonetheless, to offer the same kind of defense or justification of one's life or action or belief that is represented by a *logos*.

14. Aeschylus, *Agamemnon* 2.1388–90; all translations are from Aeschylus 2013.

15. Aeschylus, *Agamemnon* 2.1376–78.

16. Aeschylus, *Agamemnon* 2.1528–29, 1560–66.

17. Plato, *Apology of Socrates* 37d–e; Plato, *Crito* 53b–e (translation from Plato 1981).

18. This is the view promoted by Curley 1978 and Popkin 1979, among others.

19. This history is reviewed in Popkin 1979.

20. Baillet 1987, 1:162–63.

21. As he tells his friend, the Minim priest Marin Mersenne, "[T]hese six Meditations contain all the foundations of my physics" (Descartes 1991, 173 [January 28, 1641]).

22. There are many fine and highly detailed scholarly studies of the *Meditations*, including Carriero 2009; Kenny 1968; Williams 1978; and Wilson 1978.

23. Descartes's preface to the 1647 French translation (by the Abbé Picot and authorized by Descartes) of the *Principles of Philosophy* (Descartes 1984, 1:186).

24. Preface to the 1647 French translation of the *Principles of Philosophy* (Descartes 1984, 1:186).

25. *Meditations*, Synopsis (Descartes 1984, 2:9).

26. Seventh Replies (Descartes 1984, 2:324).

27. *Meditations*, First Meditation (Descartes 1984, 2:12).

28. These are the two different ways of understanding the dream argument, suggested (respectively) by how Descartes describes it in the First Meditation (Descartes 1984, 2:13) and in his recap in the Sixth Meditation (Descartes 1984, 2:53). The difference is discussed by Wilson (1978, 13–31) in her analysis of the argument.

29. *Meditations*, First Meditation (Descartes 1984, 2:13).

30. *Meditations*, First Meditation (Descartes 1984, 2:13–14).

31. *Meditations*, First Meditation (Descartes 1984, 2:14).

32. Descartes, in fact, was a fan of this sort of literature, and Cervantes's story may have played an influential role in the way in which Descartes conceived the doubts of the First Meditation; see Nadler 1997.

33. Plato, *Apology of Socrates* 21a. According to Xenophon, author of another contemporary account of Socrates's trial, what the oracle said was "Socrates is wisest" (Xenophon, *Apology of Socrates*, §14).

34. Plato, *Apology of Socrates* 21b.

35. Plato, *Apology of Socrates* 21a–d.

36. Perhaps Socrates's denials of such moral knowledge are ironic, merely pedagogical ruses to draw out his interlocutors as he seeks to discover what they know. Socrates's "irony" has long been the subject of scholarly debate; see, for example, Lane 2011; Vasiliou 2002; and Vlastos 1991.

37. Plato, *Apology of Socrates* 21d.

38. This would be what has been called the "humility theory" of wisdom: a person is wise if and only if that person believes he is not wise; see the introduction to Lehrer et al. 1996 and Ryan 2018.

Conclusion: Thinking Responsibly

1. Oreskes 2019, 71–72.
2. Oreskes 2019, 246.
3. Douglas 2009, 201.

Bibliography

Aeschylus. 2013. *The Oresteia*. Edited and translated by David Grene and Richmond Lattimore. Chicago: University of Chicago Press.

Alston, William P. 1989. *Epistemic Justification: Essays in the Theory of Knowledge*. Ithaca, NY: Cornell University Press.

Anderson, Steven, Antoine Bechara, Hanna Damasio, Daniel Tranel and Antonio R. Damasio. 1999. "Impairment of Social and Moral Behavior Related to Early Damage in Human Prefontal Cortex." *Nature Neuroscience* 2: 1032–1037.

Appiah, Kwame Anthony. 2020. "How Do I Deal with a Friend Who Thinks COVID-19 Is a Hoax?" The Ethicist, *New York Times Magazine*, April 22.

Aristotle. 1985a. *The Complete Works of Aristotle*. 2 vols. Edited by Jonathan Barnes. Princeton, NJ: Princeton University Press.

———. 1985b. *Nicomachean Ethics*. Translated by Terence Irwin. Indianapolis, IN: Hackett Publishing.

Bacon, Francis. 1939. *Novum Organon* (1620). In *The English Philosophers from Bacon to Mill*, edited by E. A. Burtt, 24–123. New York: Random House.

Baillet, Adrien. 1987. *La vie de Monsieur Descartes*. Facsimile reprint. New York, 1987. Originally published in Paris: Daniel Horthemels, 1691.

Barnes, Jonathan, ed. 1982. *The Presocratic Philosophers*. 2nd ed. London: Routledge and Kegan Paul.

Bechara, Antoine, Antonio R. Damasio, Hanna Damasio and Steven W. Anderson. 1994. "Insensitivity to Future Consequences Following Damage to Human Prefontal Cortex." *Cognition* 50: 7–15.

Benatar, David, ed. 2010. *Life, Death and Meaning*. Lanham, MD: Rowman and Littlefield.

Benson, Hugh. 2000. *Socratic Wisdom*. Oxford: Oxford University Press.

———. 2013. "The Priority of Definition." In *The Bloomsbury Companion to Socrates*, edited by J. Bussanich and N. D. Smith, 136–55. London: Continuum.

Berlin, Isaiah. 2002. *Liberty*. Oxford: Oxford University Press.

———. 2013. *The Hedgehog and the Fox: An Essay on Tolstoy's View of History*. Edited by Henry Hardy. 2nd ed. Princeton, NJ: Princeton University Press.

Broadie, Sarah. 1991. *Ethics with Aristotle*. Oxford: Oxford University Press.

Carriero, John. 2009. *Between Two Worlds: A Reading of Descartes's Meditations*. Oxford: Oxford University Press.

Chignell, Andrew. 2018. "The Ethics of Belief." *Stanford Encyclopedia of Philosophy*. Spring 2018 ed. https://plato.stanford.edu/cgi-bin/encyclopedia/archinfo.cgi?entry=ethics-belief.

Clifford, William. 1877. "The Ethics of Belief." *Contemporary Review* 29:289–309.

Cooper, John. 2012. *Pursuits of Wisdom: Six Ways of Life in Ancient Philosophy*. Princeton, NJ: Princeton University Press.

Cottingham, John. 2002. *On the Meaning of Life*. London: Routledge.

Crawford, Amanda. 2020. "The Professor of Denial." *Chronicle of Higher Education Review*, February 14.

Cummins, Eleanor. 2019. "How Autism Myths Came to Fuel Anti-Vaccination Movements." *Popular Science*, February 1.

Curley, Edwin. 1978. *Descartes against the Skeptics*. Cambridge, MA: Harvard University Press.

Damasio, Antonio R. 1994. *Descartes' Error: Emotion, Reason and the Human Brain*. New York: Putnam.

———. 1996. "The Somatic Marker Hypothesis and the Possible Functions of the Prefrontal Cortex". *Philosophical Transactions of the Royal Society of London*. Series B: Biological Sciences. **351**: 1413–1420.

Descartes, René. 1964–72. *Oeuvres de Descartes*. Edited by Charles Adam and Paul Tannery. 12 vols. Paris: J. Vrin.

———. 1984. *The Philosophical Writings of Descartes*. Vols. 1 and 2. Edited and translated by John Cottingham, Robert Stoohoff, and Dugald Murdoch. Cambridge: Cambridge University Press.

———. 1991. *The Philosophical Writings of Descartes*. Vol. 3: *The Correspondence*. Edited and translated by John Cottingham, Robert Stoohoff, Dugald Murdoch, and Anthony Kenny. Cambridge: Cambridge University Press.

Diels, H., and W. Kranz. 1974. *Die Fragmente der Vorsokratiker*. 3 vols. Berlin: Weidmann.

Dorion, Louis-André. 2011. "The Rise and Fall of the Socrates Problem." In *The Cambridge Companion to Socrates*, edited by Donald R. Morrison, 1–23. Cambridge: Cambridge University Press.

Douglas, Heather. 2009. *Science, Policy and the Value-Free Ideal*. Pittsburgh, PA: University of Pittsburgh Press.

Doyle, Arthur C. 2016a. "Silver Blaze." *The Memoirs of Sherlock Holmes*, 7–26. Ballingslöve, Sweden: Wisehouse Classics.

———. 2016b. *A Study in Scarlet*. Ballingslöve, Sweden: Wisehouse Classics.

Futter, Dylan B. 2019. "The Socratic Fallacy Undone." *British Journal for the History of Philosophy* 27:1071–91.

Geach, Peter. 1966. "Plato's *Euthyphro*: An Analysis and Commentary." *The Monist* 50:369–82.

Gettier, Edmund. 1963. "Is Justified True Belief Knowledge?" *Analysis* 23:121–23.

Gigerenzer, Gerd, and Ulrich Hoffrage. 1995. "How to Improve Bayesian Reasoning without Instruction: Frequency Formats." *Psychological Review* 102:684–704.

Ginet, Carl. 2001. "Deciding to Believe." In *Knowledge, Truth and Duty*, edited by M. Steup, 63–76. New York: Oxford University Press.

Gottlieb, Paula. 2009. *The Virtue of Aristotle's Ethics*. Cambridge: Cambridge University Press.

Hadot, Pierre. 2004. *What Is Ancient Philosophy?* Cambridge, MA: Belknap Press.

Haidt, Jonathan. 2001. "The Emotional Dog and Its Rational Tail: A Social Intuitionist Approach to Moral Judgment." *Psychological Review* 4: 814–34.

Haidt, Jonathan. 2012. *The Righteous Mind: Why Good People Are Divided by Politics and Religion*. New York: Vintage.

Hart, H.L.A. 1961. *The Concept of Law*. Oxford: Clarendon Press.

Herodotus. 1954. *The Histories*. Translated by Aubrey de Sélincourt. Harmondsworth, UK: Penguin.

Homer. 1951. *Iliad*. Translated by Richmond Lattimore. Chicago: University of Chicago Press.

Hume, David. 1978. *A Treatise on Human Nature*. Edited by L. A. Selby-Bigg. 2nd ed. Oxford: Clarendon Press.

Hutchinson, Douglas S. 1995. "Ethics." In *The Cambridge Companion to Aristotle*, edited by Jonathan Barnes, 195–232. Cambridge: Cambridge University Press.

Hviid, Anders, Jørgen Vinsløv Hansen, Morten Frisch, and Mads Melbye. 2019. "Measles, Mumps, Rubella Vaccination and Autism: A Nationwide Cohort Study." *Annals of Internal Medicine* 170:513–20.

James, William. 1956. *The Will to Believe and Other Essays in Popular Philosophy*. New York: Dover Publications.

Kahneman, Daniel. 2011. *Thinking, Fast and Slow*. New York: Farrar, Straus and Giroux.

Kekes, John. 1983. "Wisdom." *American Philosophical Quarterly* 20:277–86.

Kenny, Anthony. 1968. *Descartes: A Study of His Philosophy*. South Bend, IN: St. Augustine's Press.

Kraut, Richard. 2006. "The Examined Life." In *A Companion to Socrates*, edited by Sara Ahbel-Rappe and Rachana Kamteker, 228–42. Malden, MA: Blackwell Publishing.

———. 2007. *What Is Good and Why: The Ethics of Well-Being*. Cambridge, MA: Harvard University Press.

———. 2018. "Aristotle's Ethics." *Stanford Encyclopedia of Philosophy*. Summer 2018 ed. https://plato.stanford.edu/archives/sum2018/entries/aristotle-ethics.

Krugman, Paul. 2020. *Arguing with Zombies: Economics, Politics, and the Fight for a Better Future*. New York: Norton.

Lane, Melissa. 2011. "Reconsidering Socratic Irony." In *The Cambridge Companion to Socrates*, edited by Donald R. Morrison, 237–59. Cambridge: Cambridge University Press.

Larmore, Charles. 1987. *Patterns of Moral Complexity*. Cambridge: Cambridge University Press.

Lehrer, Keith, Jeannie Lum, Beverly Slichta, and Nicholas D. Smith, eds. 1996. *Knowledge, Teaching and Wisdom*. Dordrecht: Kluwer.

Mele, Alfred. 1999. "Aristotle on *Akrasia*, *Eudaimonia*, and the Psychology of Action." In *Aristotle's Ethics: Critical Essays*, edited by Nancy Sherman, 183–204. Lanham, MD: Rowman and Littlefield.

Mendez, Mario F. 2006. "What Frontotemporal Dementia Reveals About the Neurobiological Basis of Morality." *Medical Hypotheses* 67: 411–18.

Nadler, Steven. 1997. "Descartes's Demon and the Madness of Don Quixote." *Journal of the History of Ideas* 58:41–55.

———. 2017. "How to Fix American Stupidity." *Time*, September 12. https://time.com/4937675/how-to-fix-american-stupidity.

———. 2020. *Think Least of Death: Spinoza on How to Live and How to Die*. Princeton, NJ: Princeton University Press.

Nagel, Thomas. 1970. *The Possibility of Altruism*. Oxford: Oxford University Press.

———. 1991. *Mortal Questions*. Cambridge: Cambridge University Press.

Nickerson, Raymond. 1998. "Confirmation Bias: A Ubiquitous Phenomenon in Many Guises." *Review of General Psychology* 2:125–220.

Nozick, Robert. 1989. "What Is Wisdom and Why Do Philosophers Love It So?" In Nozick, *The Examined Life: Philosophical Meditations*, 267–78. New York: Touchstone Press.

Nussbaum, Martha. 2001. *The Fragility of Goodness: Luck and Ethics in Greek Tragedy and Philosophy*. 2nd ed. Cambridge: Cambridge University Press.

Oreskes, Naomi. 2019. *Why Trust Science?* Princeton, NJ: Princeton University Press.

Ovid. 2004. *Metamorphoses*. Translated by David Raeburn. London: Penguin.

Pascal, Blaise. 1966. *Pensées*. Translated by A. J. Krailsheimer. Harmondsworth, UK: Penguin.

Perrigo, Billy. 2020. "How Coronavirus Fears Have Amplified a Baseless But Dangerous 5G Conspiracy Theory." *TIME*, April 9.

Plato. 1961. *The Collected Dialogues of Plato*. Edited by Edith Hamilton and Huntington Cairns. Princeton, NJ: Princeton University Press.

———. 1981. *Five Dialogues*. Translated by G.M.A. Grube. Indianapolis, IN: Hackett Publishing.

Plumer, Brad, and Coral Davenport. 2019. "Science under Attack: How Trump Is Sidelining Researchers and Their Work." *New York Times*, December 28.

Pollock, John. 1986. *Contemporary Theories of Knowledge*. Totowa, NJ: Rowman and Littlefield.

Popkin, Richard. 1979. *The History of Skepticism from Erasmus to Spinoza*. Berkeley: University of California Press.

Popper, Karl. 1959. *The Logic of Scientific Discovery*. London: Hutchinson.

Railton, Peter. 1986. "Moral Realism." *Philosophical Review* 95:163–207.

Ryan, Sharon. 2018. "Wisdom." *Stanford Encyclopedia of Philosophy*. Fall 2018 ed. https://plato.stanford.edu/archives/fall2018/entries/wisdom.

Sassi, Maria Michela. 2018. *The Beginnings of Philosophy in Greece*. Princeton, NJ: Princeton University Press.

Scanlon, Thomas. 1998. *What We Owe to Each Other*. Cambridge, MA: Harvard University Press.

Sellars, Wilfrid. 1962. "Philosophy and the Scientific Image of Man." In *Frontiers of Science and Philosophy*, edited by Robert Colodny, 35–78. Pittsburgh, PA: University of Pittsburgh Press.

Shafer-Landau, Russ. 2003. *Moral Realism: A Defense*. Oxford: Clarendon Press.

Spinoza, Baruch. 1985. *The Collected Works of Spinoza*. Vol. 1. Translated by Edwin Curley. Princeton, NJ: Princeton University Press.

Stack, Liam. 2019. "Muslim Student Athlete Disqualified from Race for Wearing Hijab." *New York Times*, October 24. https://www.nytimes.com/2019/10/24/us/Ohio-hijab-runner.html.

Svavarsdóttir, Sigrún. 1999. "Moral Cognitivism and Motivation." *Philosophical Review* 108:161–219.

Tiberius, Valerie. 2008. *The Reflective Life: Living Wisely with Our Limits*. Oxford: Oxford University Press.

Tversky, Amos, and Daniel Kahneman. 1982. "Evidential Impact of Base Rates." In *Judgment under Uncertainty: Heuristic and Biases*, edited by Daniel Kahneman, Paul Slovic, and Amos Tversky, 153–60. Cambridge: Cambridge University Press.

Vasiliou, Iakovos. 2002. "Socrates' Reverse Irony." *Classical Quarterly* 52:220–30.

Vigdor, Neil. 2019. "School Security Assistant Fired for Repeating Racial Slur Aimed at Him." *New York Times*, October 18. https://www.nytimes.com/2019/10/18/us/wisconsin-security-guard-fired-n-word.html.

Vlastos, Gregory. 1991. "Socratic Irony." In Vlastos, *Socrates: Ironist and Moral Philosopher*, 21–44. Ithaca, NY: Cornell University Press.

Wainer, Howard, and Harris Zwerling. 2006. "Evidence That Smaller Schools Do Not Improve Student Achievement." *Phi Delta Kappan* 88:300–303.

Wason, Peter. 1960. "On the Failure to Eliminate Hypotheses in a Conceptual Task." *Quarterly Journal of Experimental Psychology* 12:129–40.

———. 1966. "Reasoning." In *New Horizons in Psychology*, edited by Brian Foss, 106–37. Harmondsworth, UK: Penguin.

———. 1968. "Reasoning about a Rule." *Quarterly Journal of Experimental Psychology* 20:273–81.

Wiggins, David. 1980. "Weakness of Will, Commensurability and the Objects of Deliberation and Desire." In *Essays on Aristotle's Ethics*, edited by Amélie Oksenberg Rorty, 241–66. Berkeley: University of California Press.

Williams, Bernard. 1978. *Descartes: The Project of Pure Enquiry*. Harmondsworth, UK: Penguin.

———. 1981. *Moral Luck*. Cambridge: Cambridge University Press.

Wilson, Margaret. 1978. *Descartes*. London: Routledge.

Wolf, Susan. 2010. *Meaning in Life and Why It Matters*. Princeton, NJ: Princeton University Press.

Xenophon. 1979. *Memorobilia, Oeconomicus, Symposium, Apology*. Translated by E. C. Marchant and O. J. Todd. Loeb Classical Library, no. 168. Cambridge, MA: Harvard University Press.

Index

A Note on the Type

This book has been composed in Arno, an Old-style serif typeface in the
classic Venetian tradition, designed by Robert Slimbach at Adobe.
This book also features display type set in Neue Haas Unica, a digital
revival of the 1980 neo-grotesque typeface Unica, designed by
Toshi Omagari for Monotype.